The Suryavanshis

LEGENDS OF THE IKSHVAKU DYNASTY

Tales of Shree Rama and His Ancestors

RUPESH PILLAI

ISBN
Hardcase 979-8-89498-305-9
Paperback 979-8-89475-305-8

Table of Contents

Preface

In today's world, when we look around, we see chaos; people hungry for power, engrossed in fighting among one another. There is another fight, which is within oneself in a race to accumulate materialistic pleasures. The very purpose of life has been lost, leading people to depression, aggression, anger, suicide, etc. Our history is filled with characters who will be able to inspire the generations to come out of this negative field of energy. Various Puranas, Ramayana, and Mahabharata are a few of the books which would be able to provide us with the solutions that will help us in uplifting ourselves.

Ramayana by Maharishi Valmiki is among the oldest and most inspiring epics ever written. It is our history, where the lives of Rama, Lakshmana, Sita, and many more have been told in such a way that it provides psychological, in-depth wisdom. This book is written with the intention of introducing the knowledge and wisdom provided in Valmiki Ramayana to the readers. The book also contains the history of the ancestors of Shree Rama, including Satyavrata, Harishchandra, Bhagiratha, etc. The stories help us understand the true dharma of the King, an ideal relationship that should exist between husband and wife, father and child, brothers, etc. The book gives insight into legends belonging to the Suryavanshi dynasty (solar race), a dynasty into which our Shree Rama was born. It also gives a brief insight into the age-old classic Valmiki Ramayana, which is our Iti-ha-saa (history) told in story form.

Invocations

राम रामेति रामेति, रमे रामे मनोरमे ।
सहस्रनाम तत्तुल्यं, रामनाम वरानने ॥

Raama Raama Raameti Rame Raame Manorame;
Sahasranaama Tat-Tulyam Raamanaama Varaanane.

Raghupati Raghava RajaRam,
Patheetha Paavana SitaRam.
Sundar Vigraha Meghashyam,
Ganga Thulasi Shaalighram.
Bhadra Gireeshwar SitaRam,
Bhakta Jana Priya SitaRam.
Jaanaki Ramana SitaRam,
Jaya Jaya Raaghava SitaRam.

Chapter 1

Vivasvat – The Sun God

The Beginning of Creations

In the beginning, there was only the unmanifest form of Supreme Brahman, which is formless and without any attributes. From the unmanifest form emerges the manifested form – the Saguna Brahman. Lord MahaVishnu is the form of Saguna Brahman. From the navel of Lord MahaVishnu, Lord Brahma emerged, sitting in the middle of a lotus. Lord Brahma created four kumaras – Sanaka, Sanandana, Sanatana and Sanatkumara. Lord Brahma then created ten sons through the power of His mind, and hence, they were referred to as Manasaputras. Among them was Maharshi Marichi.

Marichi married Kala and had a son named Maharshi Kashyapa. Lord Brahma created Prajapati Daksha and had many daughters from his wife, Prasuti. Of the many daughters, thirteen were married to Maharshi Kashyapa. From Aditi and Maharishi were born Devatas or Gods. Diti and Danu, other wives of Maharishi, gave birth to Daityas and fierce Danavas, respectively. From the rest of the wives were both Yakshas, Rakshasas, Nagas, Garuda, birds, and other species of animals.

The hosts of Devatas, who were characterised by goodness, were made the participators in sacrifices and rulers of the world by Lord Brahma. The hostile Daityas, Danavas, and Rakshasas started harassing the Devatas, which led to a fierce battle. In this battle, the powerful Daityas and Danavas were victorious.

As a result, the sons of Aditi were cast out and robbed of their kingdoms.

Birth of Martanda

Seeing the plight of her sons, Mother Aditi did severe penance to appease Sun by restricting her food and offering oblations to the Sun, day and night. Sun God, pleased with her dedication, appears before her, full of light and difficult to gaze at due to the halo of flame. Seeing him, Aditi said, *"Be gracious to me! I cannot gaze on you, O lord. Standing in front of you, I find it difficult to look at you as brilliant and burning as you are. O gracious, May I see your form."*

Thereupon, from his own glory, the Sun revealed himself and asked Aditi, *"Choose from me the coveted boon that you desire"*. Aditi then spoke, *"O God! Be Gracious! The mighty Daityas and Danavas have snatched from my sons the three world and their share of sacrifice. Kindly bestow on me a favour; with a portion of yourself, you enter into brotherhood with my sons and destroy their enemies so that my sons can take their share of sacrifices and become rulers of the three worlds."*

Thereupon, the Sun said, *"O Aditi, I will take birth from your womb with all my thousand portions and speedily destroy the enemies of your sons."* Saying so, The Sun vanished from her sight, and the thousand rays of the Sun incarnated in the womb of Aditi. The mother soon gave birth to a child that blazed brilliantly with glory. Kashyapa called him Martanda and said he would be the one who would defeat the asuras, the foes who carried away the shares of sacrifices. The Devatas hearing Kashyapa assembled to experience the moment. Indra then challenged the Danavas and Daityas for battle. In the middle of the battle, Martanda burnt the Daityas to ashes and helped Indra gain victory and regain their place and share of sacrifices. Martanda was named Vivasvat due to his glory and victory over Danavas and Daityas.

Story of Sanjna and Chayya

Martanda, also known as Vivasvat, The Sun God, was married to Sanjna, the illustrious daughter of Vishvakarma. From Sanjna, they had a son named Manu Vaivasvata, also known as Shraddhadeva. Sanjana also gave birth to twins named Yama and Yami. Sanjna found Vivasvat's energy so strong that she could not bear it. Through her powers, she created a shadow of her own and called her Chayya. Sanjna told Chayya, *"I shall go to my father's house, and you shall stay behind here as me and take care of my two sons and daughter as your own. Never should you divulge this secret to anyone."*

Chayya then replied, *"Not until I am caught and threatened with a curse, I shall divulge the secret. You shall go comfortably, assured of this"*. Having heard this, Sanjna left for her father's house, but her father told her to go back to her husband. Instead, she left, impersonating the form of Mare, and went to north Kurus.

Assuming Chayya was Sanjna, the adorable Sun, Vivasvat had two more sons, Savarna Manu and Shani, and a daughter, Tapti, from Chayya.

Revealing of the Truth

As her own children were born, Chayya no longer displayed the same love and affection for Sanjna's children. Vaivasvata Manu being silent person, chose to ignore this, but Yama couldn't tolerant this and raised his leg to kick Chayya. At this, Chayya cursed Yama that his leg would fall off.

Yama went to Surya and complained, *"I only threatened to kick her, but she cursed me. Does any mother ever curse her children?"* Surya replied, *"I can't undo the curse, but I will reduce its severity. The worms would take some flesh off your leg, and it would fall off to the ground. Thus, your mother's curse will also be fulfilled, and your leg will be saved."*

Sun God then confronted Chayya and asked why she did not treat all her children equally. She tried to evade the question, but when he threatened to curse her, she said that the real Sanjna had gone to her father's abode. On hearing this, an extremely angry Sun God, Martanda, went to Vishvakarma's house. Vishvakarma cooled him off by saying, *"Due to your excessive energy, Sanjna could not bear to look at you. If you permit, I shall turn your complexion favourable, then Sanjna shall be able to look at you, and both of you can reunite."* Vishvakarma then sang the hymns of the Sun, with a divine weapon, toned down the excessive splendour of the Sun. Adopting his Yogic power, Sun met his wife, who was in the form of a mare. Possessing the form of a horse, he met his wife, Sanjna. They had two sons born in this form – Ashvinikumars. The Sun and Sanjna then returned to their original form and returned and lived happily ever after.

His first son, Shraddhadeva became the Manu of the present Manvantra. Yama became the King of righteousness, Dharmaraj. Daughter Yami became the river Yamuna. His son Savarna will become the eighth Manu. His brother, Shani became the planet Saturn, Shani Dev.

Chapter 2

Vaivasvata Manu and His Progeny

Shraddhadeva, or Vaivasvata Manu as he is known, had a personality equal to that of his ancestors in every respect. He was a solver of all doubts and the Manu or ruler of present Manvantara, which is the seventh out of the fourteen Manvantara of this Kalp. As per Vedic tradition, time is endless and cyclic. The four Yugas – Satyug (Kriti Yuga), Treta Yuga, Dvapar Yug and Kali Yuga add up to one Mahayuga. Seventy-one Mahayuga combine to form one Manvantara. Seventeen such Manvantara together form a Kalp, which is equal to one day or one night of Brahma.

Vaivasvata Manu was adorned with spiritual knowledge and his mind was in perfect equilibrium in adversities as was in prosperity. Vaivasvata Manu had nine sons Ikshvaku, Nabhaga, Dhrishta, Saryati, Narishyanta, Pramashu, Rishta, Karusha and Prishadhra.

Story of Ila

With a wish to have another son, Manu carried out austerities devoted to the Varuna and Mitr Gods. However, due to some irregularities in the ritual, a daughter, Ila, was born. With the grace of Varuna and Mitr Devatas, Ila turned into a man named Sudyumna.

One day, while Sudyumna was wandering in the forest, he entered a section of the forest where no man was allowed to enter, as it was a sacred place of Lord Shiva and Devi Parvati. As soon as Sudyumna entered the region, he instantly transformed into a beautiful woman, Ila again. In this form, Ila met King Budha, son of the moon, with whom she got married and had a son named Pururavas, and thus began the lunar dynasty, Chandravanshansham.

Sage Vasishta told the sons of Manu that in order to restore Ila back to manhood, they would have to devoutly worship Lord Shiva. The brothers of Ila carried out deep penance of Lord Shiva and, being pleased with their devotion, told them that for Ila to transform into a man, Ikshvaku would have to perform Ashvamedha Yajna. The brothers carried out the Ashvamedha Yajna, and Ila had again transformed into a man. Sudyumna, in this state, had three sons – Utlaka, Gaya, and Vinata. On the insistence of Sage Vasishta, Ila was conferred the city of Pratishta, which the latter handed over to Pururavas.

Story of Prishadhra

Manu's son, Prishadhra, was entrusted with the duty of protecting cows. He vigilantly tended to the cows at night, remaining alert. One night, while it was raining heavily, he heard the herd of cows bawling and saw them running helter-skelter in the enclosure. He noticed that a powerful tiger had caught hold of one of them, and it was howling desperately.

On hearing the scream of agony, Prishadhra rushed towards it with a sword and struck the tiger. It was pitch dark, not even stars were visible due to heavy rains and dark clouds. The tiger got his ear severed but managed to escape into the woods with extreme pain. But during this course, he had accidentally chopped off the head of a cow.

The mighty Prishadhra, who unknowingly committed the crime of killing a cow, was cursed by the family Sage, *"In consequence of this, you shall not be a Kshatriya, but an absolute Shudra."* When cursed this way, the great warrior accepted it with full respect and folded hands.

He vowed to follow lifelong celibacy and surrendered himself to the Supreme MahaVishnu. Completely devoid of any attachment, with all senses under his control, he fixed his mind only on the Absolute Supreme.

Leading his life this way, he entered the forest. One day, a huge fire broke out in the forest where he was carrying out the penance. He allowed his body to be consumed by it, but in this process, his soul became one with the Brahman – the Supreme Being, the Absolute Truth.

King Saryati's Daughter Sukanya

King Saryati was the son of Manu, and a master of Vedas. It was he who had authoritatively advised the ritualistic course of the second day at the sacrifices performed by Angiras. He had a daughter named Sukanya, whose eyes were as beautiful as a pair of lotuses. Accompanied by her daughter, King one day visited the hermitage of sage Chyavana, son of Maharshi Bhrigu.

Sukanya, who was accompanied by her maids, while roaming around the trees came across an anthill. She happened to notice a pair of luminous objects in the hole of the anthill. In her childish innocence, she pricked the two bright things with a thorn and a lot of blood began to ooze through them. This caused obstruction of stool and urine of the soldiers who had accompanied the King.

Observing this, the King immediately asked his soldiers, *"Has anyone caused injury to the Sage Chyavana? Obviously, one of us has treated his hermitage disrespectfully."* Terrified, Sukanya confessed, *"Something wrong was done by me. In ignorance, I had pierced the bright objects by thorn."* In fear, the King tried to win the favour of the sage, who was buried in the anthill, by marrying off his daughter to the Sage. After the marriage, The King then took permission from the Sage and left for his capital. Princess Sukanya, having understood the mind of her short-tempered husband, tried to please him with her services.

As time passed by, one day, the two Ashvinikumar, the physician god, arrived at the hermitage. Receiving them with respect, the Sage said to them, *"As capable as you are, kindly bestow me my youth. In return, I shall bear you the Soma juice, which you are not entitled to."* Hearing this, the Ashvinikumar told the Sage to plunge into the pool created by Siddhas. The Sage entered the pool, and then from there emerged three lovely males who looked alike in appearance, adorned with a garland of flowers and earrings of gold and finely dressed. The virtuous lady, Sukanya, failed to recognise her husband among the three males and sought Ashvinikumars' help to find her husband. Pleased by her vow of fidelity, the two gods showed Sukanya, her husband, and then, taking leave from the Sage, Ashvinikumars returned to heaven.

After a few days, with the intent of performing sacrifice, King Saryati came to the hermitage, and he saw her daughter with a man who was radiating as the sun. The King was not pleased with what he saw and told her, *"Even if your husband, a sage adored by the whole world, is an old man, you should not betray him with this man. You have brought shame to the family, both to your father and your husband."* To this, the girl smiled and said, *"He is none other than your son-in-law, the son of Maharishi Bhrigu."* She then told him the whole story of how he obtained the charming appearance. Astonished and supremely gratified, the King then hugged his daughter.

Meanwhile, the Sage Chyavana with help of King Saryati, carried out the Soma sacrifice and gave a cup of Soma juice to Ashvinikumars. Enraged at this, Indra attempted to kill the Sage using Vajra, his divine weapon. Sage Chyavana, through his power paralysed Indra holding his Vajra. Finally, with the consent of other gods, Ashvinikumars were also given the share of the Soma sacrifice.

Manu's Other Progeny

The heroic dynasty of Karushas was born in Karushas. From Dhrishta originated the race of Dharshtaka, and from Ikshvaku, the solar dynasty or Suryavansham began.

Chapter 3

King Ikshvaku and His Progeny

Story of Ikshvaku and His Sons

Ikshvaku was born to Shraddhadeva Manu and founded the kingdom of Kosala. He was the first king of the Suryavanshi dynasty. He had a hundred sons of which three were most distinguished – Vikukshi, Nimi and Danda. Fifty of his sons were given the northern kingdom, while forty-eight of them were the southern. The two sons remained with him. Nimi was the founder of the Videhas dynasty.

Story of Vikukshi

One day, Ikshvaku ordered his son, Vikukshi, to bring him flesh for the sacrifice during the Ashtashraaddh for his ancestors. Agreeing to his father's order, carrying a bow and arrow, Vikukshi left for the forest to hunt animals. During this, Vikukshi got tired and hungry. He sat down and ate a hare which was being brought for the sacrifice. Being refreshed, he brought back the remaining hunted flesh for the sacrifice. Vasistha, the family priest, had been invited to the ritual, but he said, *"This flesh is impure as it had been eaten by your son."*

After having ascertained the same from his son, The King Ikshvaku, out of anger exiled his son from his land. Because of this, Ikshvaku established himself in Jnana Yoga (The Path of knowledge) and casting off his physical body, attaining what was the highest (Moksha).

Vikukshi was called Shashaadh (hare eater) after the incident. After the demise of his father, Vikukshi ruled the entire kingdom and had a son named Puranjaya.

Story of Puranjaya

During Kritayug, a fierce battle took place between the Devatas and Asuras, and the Devatas lost. They then began to worship Lord Vishnu for help. Being the eternal deity, the Primordial One, MahaVishnu told them, *"What you desire is known to me. With regards to that, hear this from me. There is a great Kshatriya king named Puranjaya, who is the son of a royal saint, Shashaad. I will incarnate a part of me into him and slay all Daityas. Hence, prepare Puranjaya for war against Daityas."*

Hearing this, the Devatas bowed down to the Supreme Vishnu, went to Puranjaya, and said, *"O Great Kshatriya, we request you to help us destroy our enemies. Please do not embarrass us by saying no."* Hearing this, Puranjaya said, *"I shall fight your enemies and help you win, only if Indra, the lord of three worlds, the performer of hundred sacrifices, agrees to carry me on his shoulders."* Hearing this, all Devatas and Indra accepted the condition.

Thereafter, Indra took the shape of a bull and held the king on his back. The King was thus named Kakutstha, as he rode on the back of a bull (kukud), and he was called Indravah, as Indra had become his vaahan (vehicle). With the strength of Vishnu, the Supreme Lord, the King Puranjaya, armed with a celestial bow, sitting on the back of the Bull, along with the army of Devatas, besieged the town of Daityas. He engaged with them in a fierce battle, and whichever Daityas dared to face him was sent to death. The Daityas, who managed to escape his flight of arrows, fled the arena and escaped to the underworld. Having conquered the splendid city and all its wealth, King Puranjaya gave it to Indra.

King Puranjaya had a son named Anena; Anena had a son named Prithu, and Prithu's son was Vishtrashva. Vishtrashva had a son, Chaandra, and Chaandra's son was Yuvanshva. Yuvanshva's son was Shaavasta, who established the city of Shaavasti. Shaavasti had a son Brihadshava and from Brihadshava was born Kuvalyaashva.

Story of Kuvalyaashva

Brihadshava had handed over the reign of his kingdom to Kuvalyaashva. Kuvalyaashva was a very righteous King and had hundreds of sons. All of them were great archers, powerful and wise.

After handing over his kingdom, Brihadshava left for the forest, where he was stopped by sage Uttanka. Uttanka, a great disciple of Sage Vega, lived on the slopes of the mountain. Uttanka said to him, *"O King, it is your duty to protect your subjects. I am unable to perform penance in peace in my hermitage in Ujjalaka. A very huge and powerful asura, Dhundu, remains hidden beneath the sands near the sea, doing severe penance for the destruction of the world. A great column of dust is raised whenever he takes a deep sigh and lets out the air. The earth shakes, and the column of dust is accompanied by flames, burning coal and smoke. Kindly slay the asura, as I am unable to stay in my hermitage."* The saintly king then replied, *"O excellent brahman, I have laid down my arms. He is my son, Kuvalyaashva, he will certainly slay Dhundu."* He directed his son, and the saintly king left for the mountains to carry out his penance.

Accompanied by the Sage and his sons, Kuvalyaashva proceeded to slay the Asura Dhundu. At the behest of Sage Uttanka and with a desire to achieve the welfare of the world, the King and his sons reached the seashore and dug out the sandy deposits. While doing this, the Asura let out fire from his mouth, and all his sons, except three Dridhashva, Chandrashva and Kapilshva, were killed. Then, the brilliant king, with immense grace, approached the powerful Asura and slayed him with all his might.

On completion of his mission, he met the Sage Uttanka. Sage Uttanka blessed him with always being victorious and perpetually righteous. To sons who were killed by Asura, he granted them a permanent abode in heaven. The King was thus called Dhundumara. Kuvalyaashva was succeeded by Dridhashva, who had a son named Haryashva. Haryashva's son was Nikumbh, and Nikhumbh's son was Amitashva. His son was Krishasva, and his son was Prasenjit. Rishi Jamadagni had married the daughter of King Prasenjit and had a son, Parashurama, the warrior, who was the sixth incarnation of Lord MahaVishnu. Prasenjit had a son named Yuvanshva.

Chapter 4

King Yuvanshva:
The Pregnant King

Yuvanshva was a great king who aspired to uphold Dharma in his kingdom. The King had many wives but no sons. He tried various methods to solve the problem. Distressed and disappointed, he, along with his wife, left for the forest and stayed with sages in their hermit to perform yajna to obtain an heir. The sages successfully performed the religious austerities. The ceremony was completed by midnight, and after placing the consecrated water in altar, the sages went off to sleep.

King awakened at night due to thirst and entered the sages' cottage to drink water. Seeing the sages fast asleep, and not wanting to disturb them, the King picked up the altar and drank the water. Unfortunately, it was the same altar which contained the enchanted water.

When the sages woke up the next morning, discovering an empty altar, they asked, *"Who drank this consecrated water? This water was meant for the King's wife, drinking which she would have given birth to a valiant son."* Hearing this, the King said, *"It was I who unknowingly drank the water."*

Having drank the enchanted water, a child was conceived in the belly of the King. As months passed, the belly grew big, and at the right time, it ripped open the right side and thus, a boy was born. Having thus been born, the Rishis were worried and said, *"Who will now nurse the child?"* At that moment, Indra appeared and said, *"He will be nursed by me, and he will be known as Mandhaata."* Indra then put the forefinger into the mouth of the child, who sucked it, and divine nectar started to flow from it. Mandhaata became a valiant King who brought the seven continents under him. It is said that – "From the rising of the sun to its setting, wherever the lights fall, the land belongs to Mandhaata."

Through the grace of God and Brahmanas, King Yuvanshva didn't die, and he attained Blessedness in that very hermitage through penance.

Chapter 5

King Mandhaata: The Legendary King

The Mighty Mandhaata

Prince Mandhaata, born from King Yuvanshva and, having tasted the nectar from the forefingers extended by Indra, became possessed of mighty strength. The whole of sacred learning, together with Vedas and Dhanurveda, the science of arms and weapons, was acquired by the masterful boy, Mandhata, by the simple and unassisted power of his thoughts. He received the bow named Ajagava, arrows with thorns and an impenetrable shield.

Young Mandhaata was placed on the throne by the celestial king, Indra himself. King Mandhaata conquered the whole world in a righteous way, became the sovereign ruler of the world, and got the title "Sarvabhauma". He governed the world in the most righteous way, and all great personalities would come to him. He thus made the world a prosperous place to live. He performed several sacrificial rites of various kinds, in which abundant gratuities were paid to the priests.

The mighty and illustrious King Mandhaata performed plenty of pious deeds and thereby attained a position alongside Indra. That learned king of unwavering virtue sent forth his authorisation and, simply by its virtue, conquered the earth, sea, gems, and all the cities in a day. The sacred grounds for various rituals he prepared were to be found all around the earth. He would donate generously to the Brahmanas. It was said that, in case of continuous drought, he would cause the rain to fall, and even Indra would be staring at him. He protected the world from harm. He was a protector of the cultured soul.

With pride in having received various boons, the mighty Rakshasa, Ravana, once challenged King Mandhaata. King Mandhaata's single handle had defeated his army of skilled warriors. A fierce battle broke out between King Mandhaata and Ravana. Unable to overpower King Mandhaata, Ravana took out his BrahmaAstra (a powerful divine weapon). To counter this, King Mandhaata placed the PushpatAstra (divine weapon of Lord Shiva) on his bow. To prevent the entire world from being destroyed by the use of the most powerful weapons in the universe, Sage Pulatsya and Gaalava had to mediate between them and force them to retract the weapons. Both the Kings then returned to the camp. Such was the might of King Mandhaata that the mightiest of the mighty Ravana also couldn't subdue him.

King Mandhaata was married to Bindumati, the daughter of Shatbindu and had three sons – Purukutsa, Ambarisha and Muchukunda and fifty daughters. Ambarisha had a son named Yuvanashva, who, in turn, had a son named Harita, from whom the Angiras Haritas descended.

Daughters of Mandhaata and Sage Saubhari

During the reign of Mandhaata, a great Sage named Saubhari was performing his austerity in water for twelve long years. In the same water, there lived a fish named Samadh with his children and grandchildren. Samad used to live happily among them, playing with them day and night. Seeing them, Sage Saubhari lost his concentration and thought to himself, "Blessed is this being, though born in this species, he is happily *able to be with his children and grandchildren. I, too, thereby desire to have children and grandchildren and play with them.*"

With the desire to find a woman for marriage, the sage came out of the water and visited the generous King Mandhaata. Hearing the arrival of the sage, the King rose from his seat, welcomed him with great respect and honour and offered him a seat. After sitting, the Sage asked the King, "*O King, I have made up my mind to get married and bestow me one of your daughters. Don't disprove my love. Anyone approaching with something to the race of Kakutstha, is never refused. There are plenty of Kings in this world, but it is your race that is firm in keeping their vows and not disappointing the person who has come to you asking for something. You have fifty daughters; I am asking to give only one among them.*"

Having heard of the Sage, looking at his old age and decaying body, and fearing the curse of the Sage, the king remained in silence for some time. Seeing this, the Sage again said, "*O King, what are you thinking about? I am not asking much. You are sure to give your daughter to someone in marriage someday. But if you fulfil my wish, there are a lot of things you can gain.*"

The King thought for a while and replied, "*O illustrious one, it is the practice in our lineage; the daughters are given to the person whom they themselves select. Your desire is not known to them, and I don't know what to do.*" The Sage then said, "*This is one way of refusing me. I am an old man, and I will not be appealed by any women, let alone your daughters. If this is so, then kindly have the eunuch guard take me to your daughter's quarters. If any girl desires me, I will marry her; otherwise, I will set aside the idea of marriage.*"

Scared of the Sage's curse, the King ordered the guards to take the Sage to the living quarters of the princesses. While entering the quarters, the Sage transformed himself into a handsome personality, exceeding that of the Siddhas and Gandharvas. The guard then spoke to the princesses, *"The illustrious king, your father has sent this pious Sage here. He wishes to marry one among you. The King has promised to him that he will be married only if he is selected by any of you."*

Seeing him, all princesses fell in love with the Sage, and each one of them wanted to marry him. There rose a conflict among them, each contending to marry him. The guard then reported the matter to the King. The King perplexed and reluctantly gave away all his daughters in marriage to the Sage. He married all of them and brought them to his hermitage.

Thereafter, the Sage summoned Vishvakarma, the creator of artisanship, to construct separate palaces for each of his wives and furnish each palace with all the richness and reservoirs of water with lotus, ducks, swans, and other birds. Vishvakarma did as had been instructed by the Sage. The palaces were filled with an abundant supply of foods, and other pleasures.

One day, King Mandhaata visited the daughters to check if they were happy or not. When he entered the Maharishi hermitage, he saw splendid palaces. He first entered the palace of his eldest daughter and enquired about her well-being. The daughter then replied, *"O father, look at this enchanting palace which possesses every kind of pleasure and happiness. There is but only one grief – my husband never goes out of my house, never goes to my sisters. He is solely attached to me."* He then entered the other palaces one by one, and every daughter had the same answer. Sage, through his power, was able to stay with all of them at the same time, and King understood this. He then met

Sage Saubhari and said to him, "*O great one, I have never seen such great power. Great is the reward of your austerity.*" King Mandhaata then honoured him and returned to his palace.

As time passed by, the princesses gave birth to one hundred and fifty sons. Saubhari's attachment to them increased day by day, and his mind became engrossed in more selfish thoughts. His desires for materialistic pleasures grew, and he started thinking about when the sons would talk, then walk, attain youth, get married and then have their children. Sage Saubhari soon realised that there is no end to desires. He thought, "*As one desire is satisfied, the other springs up. Having seen the children's children, I have always seen a new desire springing up. I have now learned that there is no end to desires. Even the most accomplished are degraded by worldly attachments. Remaining submerged in water, I had accumulated a lot of austerities. My association with the fish first destroyed the same thing, and then my attachment to my children. I now seek refuge in the Supreme Vishnu, who is the teacher of teachers, the eternal lord.*"

Thinking so, fixing his mind on the Supreme being, he, along with his wives, left for the forest. There, in the forest, he performed severe austerities to cleanse himself of the sins. He, surrendering all his actions to the Supreme Lord, attained Moksha.

Story of Muchukunda

Born in the race of Ikshvaku, son of Mandhaata, Muchukunda was a great warrior and pious man. During the war between the Devatas headed by Indra and Asura, Indra sought the help of King Muchukunda. Having secured the service of Karthikeya, son of Lord Shiva, Indra expressed their gratitude to the King who had travelled to Swarga to protect them. He said, "*O King, you may now retire from the tiring task of protecting us. Having given up your kingdom, you have been protecting us, and in doing so, you have given up all your pleasures."*

They also revealed that during this period, an entire yuga passed and is presently transitioning into Dvapar Yuga. All his family members have long deceased. They also offered to ask Muchukunda for any boon except for Moksha, which was beyond their capacity. Muchukunda then respectfully bowed to the Devatas, who wished to grant him undisturbed sleep. The Devatas then assured him, *"He who would thoughtlessly wake you up from your sleep will be turned to ashes the very moment you are awakened."* The King then went to a cave and commenced his sleep.

Once Kalayavana, a mighty Danav warrior who had no rivals among men, was undefeated in battle due to a boon from Lord Shiva. Allied with King Jarasandha of Magadha kingdom, whom Shree Krishna had defeated seventeen times, he laid siege to the kingdom of Mathura. Shree Krishna did not kill Kalayavana due to the boon he had received from Lord Shiva. During the battle, Shree Krishna got down from the chariot and began to retreat. Kalavayana followed Shree Krishna as he was running away. Shree Krishna lured him into the same cave where Muchukunda had been sleeping. Kalayavana saw someone sleeping inside the cave, and assuming him to be Shree Krishna, Kalayavana struck him on his foot. Opening his eyes slowly, King Muchukundu gazed upon Kalavayana, who was immediately reduced to ashes.

Shree Krishna then revealed himself to King Muchukunda and told King Muchukundu to perform severe penance because, as a part of his duties as Kshatriya, he had killed many living beings. In the next birth, Muchukunda will be born as Brahmana and a friend of all living beings and then will attain Moksha.

Having been blessed this way, King Muchukundu stepped out of the cave and found that the stature of all creatures had shrunk as Kali Yug had set in. Endowed with faith, the wise king concentrated on the Supreme Being and went to Gandamadana mountain and from there reached Badhrika Ashram, the abode of Nara and Narayana. With his mind fixed on the Supreme Hari, he continued his austerities.

Chapter 6

King Purukutsa and His Descendants

King Purukutsa and Nagas

Once in the world of Rasatalas, regions below the earth, sixty million Gandharvas lived named Mauneyas. They had taken control of the land of Nagas and seized upon the precious jewels of Nagas, thereby depriving them of their rights. Distressed with the situation, the Naga chiefs prayed to the Supreme God, MahaVishnu, for help. Pleased with their prayers, the Supreme God opened his lotus eye and said, *"O God, how shall we be free from this fear?"* The Supreme God then said, *"I shall infuse my energy into the person named Purukutsa, son of Mandhaata and subdue these Gandharvas."*

On hearing these words from the Supreme God, the Nagas bowed to Him, returned to their country and sent Narmada to secure the help of Purukutsa. Narmada was the sister of the Naga chief and was married to Purukutsa. Accordingly, Narmada went to Purukutsa, led him to the world below, and explained the entire situation to him. Purukutsa, infused with the energy of MahaVishnu, destroyed all the Gandharvas and captured the world of Nagas back from Gandharvas, gave it to the Nagas, and returned home.

The Naga gods conferred upon Narmada a boon that whosoever should think of her, mention her name, should have no fear from snakes. They also conferred a boon on Purukutsa that no one in his family shall ever be bitten.

Purukutsa from his wife Narmada, had a son named Trasadasya, who had a son named Sambhuta. The son of Sambhuta was Anaranya.

Story of Anaranya

Anaranya, the King of Ayodhya, was a great scholar and master of weapons. During this period, Ravana had been terrorising the kings around the world, many of them had submitted without any resistance.

Ravana, who had received a boon from Lord Brahma, said that anyone born in the race of devas, asuras, Danavas, yakshas, nagas, etc., could ever harm him. Out of arrogance, he never included humans in the boon, as he thought humans were not strong enough to even hurt him. He then attacked all the worlds and defeated all devas, Danavas, yakshas, etc. Finally, he started his conquest of the earth. He had challenged King Anaranya of Ayodhya to surrender, but the King had other ideas.

A fierce battle broke out between the two, in which King Anaranya lost all his army to Ravana. During the battle, King Anaranya was fatally injured by Ravana. Ravana then asked King Anaranya what he had gained from the battle; he would have lived longer if he had surrendered. The King replied it was his fate that killed him and not the weapons of Ravana. He cursed Ravana that a descendant of his race would kill Ravana in the future.

King Anaranya's son was Prishadshva, and his son was Hariyashva and Sumanas. The son of Sumanas was Tridhanvan. He was succeeded by his son Trayyaruna. Trayyaruna had a son named Satyavrata.

-33-

Chapter 7

King Satyavrata: The Over-Ambitious King

Battle of Superiority

A long time ago, King Vishvamitra set out into the forest for a hunting expedition. After spending long hours in the forest, the exhausted King and his troops reached the hermitage of Sage Vasishta. The Sage welcomed the guests and gave the King and his troops a grand feast. The King then enquired with the Sage about how he could manage such a grand feast in such a short time. Sage then told him that it was with the help of the divine cow Sabala. Seeing this, the King wanted the possession of the cow and, in return, was ready to reward him handsomely, but the Sage refused. The soldiers tried to forcibly take the cow. Hundreds of warriors sprung out from the cow and fought the army. With his yogic powers, the Sage uttered a mantra, and the King's army turned into ashes and defeated King Vishvamitra.

Embarrassed by the defeat, The King handed over the throne to his sons and, along with his wife, entered the forest in the south and undertook the most rigid austerities to obtain divine weapons. Lord Shiva granted him the boon of knowledge of divine weapons. Using the newly acquired weapons, he destroyed Sage's hermitage, which caused Sage Vasishta to be angry and challenge Vishvamitra. During the dual, none of

Vishvamitra's weapons could harm Sage. Seeing the power of a Brahmarishi, Vishvamitra fled the place and was determined to become a Brahmarishi himself. As years passed, Lord Brahma appeared before Vishvamitra and granted him Rajarishi status due to the severe austerities he had been performing. But Vishvamitra was not happy with this, as he wanted to be Brahmarishi, so he started doing even greater penances and austerities.

King Satyavrata's Extra-ordinary Wish

Satyavrata, son of Trayyaruna, ascended the throne of Kosala, Ayodhya. He ruled the kingdom following dharma and self-restraint. Sage Vasishta was his royal chief priest. Satyavrata was married to Sathyaratha and born into the Kaikeya family. They had a son, Harishchandra, who was sinless.

As the prince grew older and eligible, King Satyavrata crowned him as the King. King Satyavrata had a strange wish wherein he wanted to enter Heaven with his mortal body. He approached Sage Vasishta to help him perform a sacrifice to achieve this. But Sage Vasishta refused to perform the yajna and told him that going to heaven with the mortal body is against the laws of nature and he should abstain from doing so. But the King was adamant and approached the sons of Vasishta. He told them his intent, but they were annoyed.

The sons of Sage Vasishta said angrily, "*O Foolish minded, you have been refused by your Guru, who is truthful; how could you bypass him and approach us? Guru had been the chief priest of the Ikshvaku dynasty, and it is not right to bypass him. When he refused, how could we make the sacrifice? O King, you are being childish; return to your capital. Sage Vasishta can only perform such sacrifices; how can we dishonour him.*"

ॐ

Having heard this, the King again said, *"Having rejected by my Guru and his sons, I shall seek another way."* Having seen his strong intent, the Sage's sons were furious and cursed him to be Chandaal. That night, the King's body was transformed into a dark-complexioned, dirty man with a disgusting appearance. His body was smeared with ashes from the cemetery and soiled clothes. Seeing their king in this form, all his councillors and citizens moved away from him. Thus, in distress, the king started wandering in the forest and soon reached Sage Vishvamitra.

King Satyavrata Meets Sage Vishvamitra

On seeing the King in the present form, Sage Vishvamitra was touched with pity and asked him, *"O Mighty One, are you the King of Ayodhya? Whose curse has turned you into a Chandaal?"* The King then respectfully explained the entire episode to the Sage Vishvamitra. He also told the Sage about his intention of entering Swarga with his physical body and requested his help in fulfilling his wish. The Sage Vishvamitra, who was Sage Vasishta's rival, replied, *"O child, I know that you are righteous. O Eminent among Kings, don't fear! I shall offer you refuge. I shall invite the pious maharishis to assist you in your yajna (sacrifice), and with the present body, disfigured by the curse, you shall go to heaven."*

Vishvamitra then ordered his sons to prepare for the yajna and bring other rishis along with their disciples for the same. Sage Vishvamitra then addressed the Rishis present there to join in the performance of yajna so that Satyavrata could reach heaven. Fearing Vishvamitra's anger, all rishis joined him in the yajna. On completion of the yajna, Sage Vishvamitra invoked the gods to partake in the offerings of yajna. When the Devatas did not come to receive the share of their offering, the angry Vishvamitra said to Satyavrata that he would go to heaven with the physical body. He used all his spiritual power to raise Satyavrata in Swarga.

Becoming Trishanku

On seeing ascendance of Satyavrata, Indra, the king of gods said that the cursed one cannot enter the Swarga and pushed him down to earth. Satyavrata started to descend with his head down and he started crying, "*O Great Rishi Vishvamitra, please protect me.*" Having heard kings cry, Vishvamitra was able to halt the descend and king was left suspended mid-way. The Sage then created a new constellation in the south for the king.

Seeing Vishvamitra's anger and power of austerities, Indra told the Sage that the king who has been cursed by his guru is not worthy of going to heaven, and also, it is against nature for someone to enter heaven with his physical body. Sage then said that he does not wish to go back on his promise made to the King. So, the Sage created a new world with planets and stars. So, Indra let the new constellation created for the king be his heaven, and all other gods gave their consent. Thus, amidst those stars, King Satyavrata remained immortal and suspended with his head downwards. Being stuck between the heaven and earthly plane in a new constellation, King Satyavrata came to be known as Trishanku.

Chapter 8

King Harischandra: The Curse of God Varuna

Boon from God Varuna

King Harishchandra, who had ascended the throne of Ayodhya, was a virtuous soul and a great king whose subjects enjoyed peace and prosperity. The king was married to a beautiful and clever wife, Shaivya. The only sorrow in his life was that they never had a son. So, the King shared his mental agony with Sage Vasishta. Sage Vasishta advised the King to worship God Varuna (God of water) for the same.

The King, following the words of the Brahmarishi, bowed with respect, went to the bank of river Sarayu and performed severe austerities devoted to God Varuna. God Varuna, delighted with King's austerities and worship, said, *"O King! I am satisfied with your tapasya, so ask for a boon."* King then replied, *"I am without a son; grant me a boon to have a son, who will free me from the debts of Devatas, Pitrs and Rishis."* God Varuna smiled and said, *"I will grant you a well-deserved qualified son, but in return, you will need to fearlessly sacrifice your son after he crosses the first ten days of his life in honour of me."*

The King agreed to this condition. God Varuna then blessed him and disappeared. After a few days, Queen Shaivya was pregnant and gave birth to a boy, Rohitasva. On his birth, the joyous King performed all the ceremonies and distributed wealth and jewels as his joy knew no bounds. God Varuna appeared after ten days and demanded the sacrifice which was promised by the King. The King requested God Varuna to let the child be one month so he would be ready for sacrifice. God Varuna acknowledged and left, but he returned after one month had passed and asked for the pledged sacrifice. The King kept postponing his sacrifice citing various reasons.

Curse of God Varuna

When the child was ten years old, God Varuna appeared before the King and requested for the pending sacrifice. King said he would oblige with the sacrifice after the Samavartana ceremony (i.e. when the student returns from gurukul after completion of his education). God Varuna then said, *"O King, you are very much attached to your son and have been repeatedly deceiving me for various reasons. Today, I will go back but will surely return at the time of the Samavartan ceremony."*

Prince Rohitasva was intelligent and had seen the God Varuna visiting the King frequently. He understood that he would be offered as sacrifice soon as per the promise made. Rohitasva then left the city and went to a deep forest. The King sent his people in search of the prince but all in vain. As time arrived, God Varuna returned and enquired about his sacrifice. The King said that his son has gone missing and had been searching for him everywhere without any luck.

God Varuna was very angry at the King for being unable to keep up his words. In anger, he cursed the king to be infected with dropsy (a disease in which body tissues or body cavity is accumulated with water and oedema) and suffer severe pain.

The King soon was infected with dropsy. As the days passed by, his pain kept increasing and becoming unbearable.

Sacrifice of Shunashepha

The prince, on the other hand, hearing his father's condition, desired to meet him. As he was about to visit his father, Indra came and stopped him and told him to remain in the forest for one more year. Disguised as Brahman, Indra would repeatedly stop him from going to his father every year.

The King, who was affected by the disease, asked Sage Vasishta for a remedy. The Sage replied, *"O King! Purchase a boy by giving his value and make him your son and then offer him as you promised. There surely would be a Brahmin in your kingdom who will be ready to sell his son to you."*

Hearing this, the King ordered his councillors to look out for the same. After a prolonged search, they found a Brahmin named Ajigarta, who was very poor and had three sons – Shunahpuccha, Shunashepha and Shunolangula. King requested the Brahmin to sell one of his sons, and in return, he would be granted one hundred cows. Ajigrata, who was in dire straits for food and, after deep thought, decided to sell his second son, Shunashepha.

The child was brought before the King, and all preparations were made to prepare for his sacrifice. The boy trembled and cried; the slaughterer, too, hesitated. Seeing this, Ajigrata himself moved forward to kill his own son. As he was about to be killed, Sage Vishvamitra arrived at the scene and went to the King and said that this Brahmin must be a demon in the human body and asked what happiness the Brahmin would derive from wealth so accumulated by slaughtering his own son.

Vishvamitra further said, "*Let the boy who is crying piteously be freed, and there is no vice in killing someone as pure as the boy. He who wants his own welfare must not slay any other being. You must treat all being like yourself. If anyone kills another person without any enmity, then the killed will certainly come after the slayer in the next life. When one performs Ashvamedha Yajna, he will certainly have sons. I request you to free this boy, and if you do not keep my word, you will incur sin.*"

The King then told the Sage that he is suffering from dropsy due to the curse from God Varuna for not fulfilling the promise. Hence, he will not be able to free the boy. Sage Vishvamitra then went to the child and gave him Varuna Mantra.

As soon as he pronounced the Mantra, God Varuna appeared, and everyone was glad to see him. King fell on his feet and began to sing hymns to God Varuna, saying, "*O Deva, my intellect is very much tainted, and I am a sinner before you. O Merciful One, show me mercy and sanctify my humble self. I disregarded your words. Kindly show mercy on me. You are wise, and I am ignorant. For your satisfaction, I had purchased a boy and commenced your sacrifice. Your sight has taken away my infinite troubles; if you are pleased, free me from this disease.*"

God Varuna took pity on him and spoke, "*O King, Shunashepha is uttering hymns of me and is distressed. Let go of him. Your sacrifice is accomplished, and you will be free from the disease.*" God Varuna freed the King from his disease. Shunashepha also was freed and pacified. Shunashepha then asked, "*Whose son am I now? Who is my respectful father? Please advise me, and I shall oblige.*" It was then decided on merits that since Sage Vishvamitra was the one who had saved the boy, the boy became the son of Vishvamitra.

ॐ

King Harishchandra promised to be truthful to his word henceforth. By this time, Rohitasva had also returned home and cried before his father. His father gladly welcomed him and embraced him. The king and the prince then began to govern their kingdom together in the most righteous ways.

Chapter 9

King Harischandra:
The Truthful King

Sage Vishvamitra's Test

The King Harishchandra once performed Rajasuya yajna in which the Sage Vashishta was honoured. He distributed abundant wealth was bestowed to all the Sages who visited him.

When Sage Vasishta visited Swarga, he started to praise King Harishchandra. He said that the King was very righteous and that after the Rajasuya Yajna, he gave abundant Dakshinas to all. He said the King was virtuous and charitable and took care of his people. Hearing this, Sage Vishvamitra was angry and said, *"He had cheated the God Varuna after receiving the boon. He was a liar and a cheat. He had put an innocent child for sacrifice for his personal gain. I will test him for his virtuousness and charity."*

One day, while hunting in the forest, the King heard the voice of a woman screaming for help. King immediately approached her and said that there was a Sage who was doing very severe austerities, and it was troubling her. The King immediately approached the Sage, who was none other than Sage Vishvamitra himself. He requested him to stop the austerities, and in return, he would give him anything he desired. This angered the Sage, and he asked the King for his entire kingdom, his troops, his gold and all his fortune, except his wife and son. The King obliged and gave everything to the Sage.

On receiving the gifts, the Sage Vishvamitra then asked for Dakshina for the Rajasuya Yajna, which the King had performed. The King then replied, *"O Muni, this kingdom and the entire fortune have been given to you. I am only left with these bodies (himself, his wife and son)."* The Sage then said, *"Nevertheless, you must give me my Dakshina; a promise unfulfilled, especially to Brahmins, is sinful."* King then replied, *"O Adorable One, I have nothing with me now; you must give me a month's time, and I will give you your Dakshina."* The Sage Vishvamitra agreed and bowed with respect; the King then left.

The King Sells His Queen and Son

The King, along with his wife and son, left the city of Ayodhya and reached Banaras, the city of Lord Shiva and Parvati, by walk. The journey was long, and slowly, one month passed by. On the last day of the month, they saw the Sage Vishvamitra, who told the King, *"You had promised that you would pay the Dakshina by the end of one month; today is the end of the month."* The King replied, *"O wise one, one month is not complete yet. Still half a day is remaining; wait till then."*

The King was deeply immersed in thoughts of how to pay the Dakshina. The virtuous Queen told him, *"O Maharaja, preserve your truthfulness. Sell me for the money value and give the money so gained as Dakshina to the Brahmin."* Hearing this, the King fainted, and upon regaining his consciousness, he wept and became reluctant to execute the plan. Seeing the plight of her husband, the queen, full of sorrow, tried convincing him. The young boy was dreadfully hungry and was begging his father and mother for food.

As the sun began to set, Sage Vishvamitra appeared before them and asked for his Dakshina. At that moment, an aged Brahmin appeared before the King and said, *"Give this slave girl to me; I am a purchaser and, in return, will pay you money. I have a wife who cannot do household duties, so take this money and hand over her to me as a maid."* King Harishchandra's mind was torn with grief and did not reply. The Brahmin gave the money and dragged the queen. The young boy, Rohitashva, was clutching her by his hand and started weeping.

The Queen then spoke to the Brahmin that she would not be able to perform her duties diligently if the child was separated from her. The Brahmin then paid additional money to the King and took his son also with him. Vishvamitra then again appeared before the King and demanded wealth. The King then delivered the money to him. Sage Vishvamitra then said that the Dakshina cannot be so small, considering his stature, and hence, the King should provide him with more.

Becoming Slave

The King, engraved in deep fear and sorrow, with his face hung downwards, spoke aloud, "Whoever desires me as a slave can buy me for money while the sun is still shining." Lord Yama (God of Dharma), disguised as a Chandaal, arrived there and said, *"I am in urgent need of a servant; I will keep you as my slave, tell your price."* The King then enquired about him. The Chandaal replied, *"I am the famous Chandaal, Pravira, and you will remain subject to me to collect clothes of dead persons."*

King refused to be the slave of Chandaal. Sage Vishvamitra came there and asked angrily the reason. King then replied, *"I am born of Suryavanshi race and a Kshatriya. How can I accept the slavery of Chandaal."* The angry Sage then said, *"You must give me my Dakshina, be it from Chandaal or Brahmin. Otherwise, I will put you under a curse."* The King then told him, *"O Great, I am humiliated and distressed. In lieu of my remnant Dakshina, I will be your obedient slave, I will work for you and follow your orders."*

On hearing this, Sage Vishvamitra said that he would have to obey all his commands. The king was glad to hear this and agreed to it. Sage Vishvamitra then turned to Chandaal and said, *"Come to me and give me the price of this slave. I am handing over this slave to you. I need money and not a slave."* The Chandaal, filled with joy, said he was relieved that he got the slave. King, with no sign of unpleasantries on his face, said, *"Sage Vishvamitra is my master, and I will do any work that he puts me in as now I am no more a Kshatriya."*

Sage Vishvamitra, on receiving the money, told the King that he was now free from the debt of Dakshina that he was promised and told the King to work of Chandaal. King Harishchandra was then taken by Chandaal to his house, where he was chained and beaten. King stayed there and wept for his loved ones. Later he became a gatherer of garments from dead bodies on the burning ground and followed the orders of Chandaal.

Death of Rohitashva

Meanwhile, somewhere close to Kashi, one day, the boy Rohitashva, while playing with other boys, was bitten by a deadly snake, and he died instantly. The other boys gave this news to his mother, who was a servant of the Brahmin. She, on hearing this, fell unconscious. The Brahmin sprinkled water on her face and scolded her in anger. She told him that her son was dead and begged him to be gracious. She told him that she would like to go and see her son. After prolonged pleading, the Brahmin allowed her to go to her son but told her to complete the last rites quickly and to be back by morning for the work.

The Queen ran to her child and wept endlessly. The Queen took the child and arrived at the burning ground, where she told the King that her child had died and needed to be cremated. The King and Queen didn't recognise each other. The King saw the boy, recognised him, and started crying. The King then told the story of how he reached there. The Queen also explained the story of the death of their son.

The Truth Revealed

The King and Queen decided to burn themselves in the fire along with the son. The King then prepared a funeral pile and placed his son on it. He and his wife, with folded hands, meditated on the Supreme Soul.

Just when King engaged in meditation, Indra, Yama and all other Devatas, along with Vishvamitra, arrived there and said, *"The three worlds have been won by you, your wife and your son."* Yama said, *"I am Dharma, and I am satisfied by your patience, tolerance, control of your senses and Satvik qualities."* Indra then sprinkled holy water on his son, destroying the fatal effects of the snake's poison and bringing him back to life. King and Queen also regained their former beautiful appearance. Indra then said that due to the meritorious deeds, they can ascend to heaven.

The King then replied that he was still the slave of Chandaal and was not free from his bondage. Yama revealed to the King, *"I was the Chandaal, and it was me who came as the Brahmin and took away your wife as a slave. The poisonous snake who bit your son was also me."* The King then said they alone could not go to heaven as the subjects of his kingdom were mourning due to the separation, and he could not abandon them. The King, queen, prince, the Devatas and Sage Vishvamitra all reached Ayodhya. Indra told the subjects that all the citizens can ascend to heaven.

Hearing these words of Indra, the people who were engaged in worldly desire, handed over their charge to sons and geared up to go to heaven. The King then installed his son, Rohitashva on the royal throne and took leave. There was no King like King Harishchandra and nor shall one ever be.

King Rohitashva had a son named Harita. Harita's son was Chunchu, who had two sons, Vijaya and Sudeva. The son of Vijaya was Ruruka. King Ruruka was crowned as the King of Ayodhya. He was a great king and an expert in matters pertaining to religion and wealth. Vrika was born to King Ruruka and took over the prosperous kingdom of Ayodhya. King Bahu, the son of Vrika, succeeded him and began to rule the kingdom.

Chapter 10

King Sagara:
One Born with Poison

Birth of Sagara

King Bahu was good and righteous king, who ruled the earth in best possible way. He ensured all varnas of the society performed the duties without deviation. The people in his kingdom were very happy and there was rains as required, with no famines or floods. As time passed, the power got into his head, and he started thinking himself to be superior. He forgot his spiritual duties and got deviated from his righteous path.

Once, the kingdom was attacked by Kshatriyas – Haihaya and Taalajangh, aided by the Shakas, Yavanas, Paradas, Kambojas and Pahlavas. Together, they defeated King Bahu and took away his kingdom. The King then fled to the forest along with the two queens. Queen Yadavai was pregnant while they were fleeing to the forest. The other queen got jealous of her and one day gave her poison. Because of the effect of poison, the child was confined to the womb and was not delivered for a long period of time.

King Bahu, as he traversed the forest, people started to hide from him, and he grew remorseful of his past deed. Unhappy and with no desire to live, King made his way to the hermitage of Sage Aurva. Soon, the king died of deteriorating health and old age. Having constructed the funeral pile for her husband,

Queen Yadavai decided to commit suicide in the same fire lit for her husband's funeral. At that very moment, the knower of past, present and future, Sage Aurva, came out of his hermitage and said, *"Hey, pure lady, don't commit this sinful act. There in your womb lies the heroic king, who would be king of the entire world, extremely powerful and valiant, destroyer of enemies and performer of numerous sacrifices."*

Thus, addressed by the Sage, the Queen gave up her idea of committing suicide. The Sage then took her to his hermitage and treated her. After some time, the Queen gave birth to a bright boy and with him came out the poison. All Vedic rituals were performed by the Sage, who then named the child "SAGARA" (sa – with and gara – poison). Later, after performing the upanayana ceremony, the Sage taught him Vedas and the art of warfare along with knowledge of weapons, especially AgniAstra, named Bhargav.

The Undisputed King

As the boy grew older, he asked his mother, *"O mother! Why are we living here? Who is my father, and where is he?"* The mother then told her son the entire episode. Enraged on hearing this, he promised to recover his father's kingdom and destroy the Haihaya and Taalajangh.

Young Sagara learned about Sage Vasishta, his father's chief priest. He met Sage Vasishta, who blessed him and gave him many weapons, which caused him to become invincible. When Sagara was ready to take on his enemies, he attacked and defeated the Haihaya and Taalajangh. He then defeated the Shakas, Yavanas, Paradas, Kambojas and Pahlavas and was about to kill them all. But the kings escaped and took refuge under Sage Vasishta. Sage Vasishta persuaded King Sagara not to kill his enemies. The King agreed and, instead of killing enemies, left distinguishing marks on them.

King Sagara shaved the head of Shakas partially, while Yavanas and Kambhojas had their head completely shaven. The Pahlavas were instructed to grow moustaches and beards. They were deprived of the Vedic studies and were deprived of performing religious rites. The King then also defeated the Konasarpas, the Mahishakas, the Darvas, the Cholas and the Keralas. Having thus recovered his kingdom, Sagara established his rule over the seven continents.

Birth of Asmanjas and Sixty Thousand Sons

King Sagara was married to two wives – Sumati, daughter of Sage Kashyap and the other to Kesini, daughter of King of Vidharbha. But the king didn't have any offspring and hence performed deep austerities with the help of Sage Aurva. Sage Aurva, on completion of the sacrifice, said, *"One queen will bear a child who will be responsible for the continuation of the race, and other will have sixty thousand sons endowed with fame and great determination. The queens can make their own choice among these two boons."* Kesini chose to have one son, while Sumati chose to have sixty thousand sons.

After the lapse of time, Kesini gave birth to a son named Asmanjasa, while Sumati gave birth to a gourd-like foetus, which burst open, and sixty thousand sons emerged.

Story of Asmanjasa

Asmanjasa was very wicked boy from beginning. Asmanjasa showed himself outwardly as unreasonable. King Sagara guided him in all possible ways so that he amends his ways.

They expected him to improve as he grows up but in vain. Asmanjasa gets married to Ambujakshi and has a son named Anshuman. King Sagara expected him to behave maturely, but still, there was no change in his behaviour.

Asmanjasa was in his previous birth a yogi, who got deviated from his yogic path due to an evil association and is born again with recollection of past life. He used hurl children into the river Sarayu and harass people. Thereafter the citizens of his kingdom pleaded to King Sagara to help them. King Sagara then ordered to banish the prince Asmanjasa from his kingdom.

Asmanjasa accepted the Kings order, setting aside his parental affection and leaves the kingdom. But while going he used his yogic power and restored the life into dead children whom he had thrown into the Sarayu River. Having all their children returned alive, the people of Ayodhya are astonished. The King Sagara was filled with regret.

The Sixty Thousand Sons

While Kesini had given birth to Asmanjasa, Sumati had given birth to the gourd-like foetus, which burst open, and sixty thousand sons emerged. Nurses placed all of them in pots with clarified butter and fostered them. They attained adolescence after a long time. As time passed, the sixty sons of Sagara attained youth and beauty. The sixty thousand sons were influenced by Asmanjasa's wicked behaviour.

The sixty thousand sons of King Sagara, having traversed the path of Asmanjasa, a path devoid of any virtue, were creating havoc in the world. They were terrible and ruthless and had been harassing the people, the Devatas, Gandharvas, etc. Then, all the harassed beings, along with Devatas, took shelter under Brahma.

Brahma then said, *"Hey, Devatas and all other people, kindly go back just the way you had come here. In a few days, for all the sins he committed, they will all be destroyed."* Hearing these, all the people and Devatas returned.

King Sagara and the Ashvamedha Yajna

As time passed, one day, the Great King Sagara decided to undertake the Ashvamedha Yajna, the horse sacrifice. After the rituals, the horse was allowed to wander along the length and breadth of the land. The horse was protected by the sons of the King.

On the concluding day of a fortnight, the horse, although guarded by his sons, suddenly vanished. Presuming that the horse had been stolen, the sons returned to the King and said, *"Our horse has been stolen. It is nowhere to be seen."* Hearing this, the King said, *"All of you go in different directions, every sea, island, forest, and search for the missing horse."*

The sons of the King went in all directions and started searching every forest, island, and inch of the earth until they all met each other again. The sons then returned to King and said, *"O Dear King, as per your orders, we searched every land, sea, river, islands, hills, valleys, caves, etc. But we could neither find the horse nor the thief."*

The King became anxious and angry and told his sons, *"Go and search for the horse again everywhere. Don't come back until you find the horse."*

Hearing these words of their father, the sons started the search again. After a long search, they found a rift on the surface of the earth, near the ocean. As the sons began to dig the pit in all directions, using spades and pickaxes, it caused terrible destructions all around. Various living beings including demons, nagas, rakshasas were being brutally killed and harassed by the sons of Sagara, assuming them to be the thief of the horse.

The sons of King Sagara went on digging the ocean, but the horse was nowhere to be found. Thousands of beings were cut, bruised, skins peeled off. Time kept passing, and the sons were digging with wrath, and then finally, towards the northeastern region of the sea, they saw their white horse roaming around. And near the horse was sitting the great Muni Kapila, meditating with radiance like the flames of fire.

Delighted on seeing the horse, as fate would have it, the sons of King Sagara ran forward towards the horse without paying any heed or respect to the Magnanimous Muni.

Angered at the sons of King Sagara, Sage Kapila, who was the form of Lord MahaVishnu himself, he gazed upon them. Such was the fury of the gaze that the princes were immediately burnt into ashes. Such was the intensity of the flames that all Nagas who lived in the underworld fled away.

Chapter 11

King Anshuman and the Great Sage Kapila

Prince Anshuman Meets Sage Kapila

Sage Narada visited King Sagara and broke the news of the demise of his sons. King Sagara learned about the death of his sixty-thousand valiant sons and was distressed. But he had to get back the horse to complete his sacrifice. Asmanjasa had a son named Anshuman, who was very virtuous.

The King summoned his grandson, Anshuman and said, *"My valiant sixty thousand sons laid down their lives for me. They were burnt down by Kapila Muni's anger. For the sake of the citizens of my kingdom, I banished my son and your father, Asmanjasa. You are valiant and have acquired knowledge in various fields. You are illustrious like your ancestors. Thus, O grandson! Stuck in grief and baffled by obstruction to my religious rites as I am, you must bring back the horse and prevent me from hell. Creatures in the deep are powerful, so carry your weapons. Honour those who deserve it, and kill those who obstruct the sacrifice. Come back with your mission accomplished."*

Hearing these words of his grandfather, the prince immediately left carrying his bow. The prince reached the spot where the earth was excavated by King Sagara and saw Sage Kapila sitting in meditation and the horse grazing in his vicinity.

On seeing the Great Kapila, the prince bowed down with respect and very politely narrated the reason for his arrival. The great Sage was very pleased with the prince and told the prince to ask for a boon. Prince Anshuman then said that he would need the horse for the completion of his grandfather Ashvamedha's Yajna. He also prayed for the liberation of the souls of his uncles.

The Illustrious Sage then replied, *"This is the horse you are looking for. Give it to your grandfather to complete the sacrifice. River Ganga, the purifier of three worlds, will sanctify your uncle's soul. But she has to be brought down to the earth from heaven by worshipping the Lord Shiva and the Holy Ganga. My blessings are with you."*

Crowning of Prince Anshuman

Anshuman circumambulated the Sage Kapila and, bowing down to him brought the sacrificial horse to the kingdom. On reaching the palace, Prince Anshuman fell on the feet of King Sagara with respect and then narrated the entire event to his grandfather. King heard this and no longer grieved upon his sons. He honoured the prince and completed the Ashvamedha Yajna.

The King ruled the kingdom for few more years and then entrusted the throne to his highly virtuous grandson Anshuman. King Sagara, who overcame all cravings and bonds of attachments, attained the highest Purushartha – Moksha. Anshuman following the footstep of his grandfather ruled the world in the most virtuous ways.

Chapter 12

King Bhagiratha
and the Descent of River Ganga

Story of Dilipa

King Anshuman was a great monarch and had an equally great son named Dilipa. Dilipa was a celebrated and virtuous prince, like his father and was well-versed in all scriptures. Once boy was old enough and experienced to be crowned as king, Anshuman renounced the kingdom making Dilipa as his successor. Anshuman then performed rigid austerities and penance on the mountains of Himalayas, with desire to bring Ganga on to the earth. But he was unsuccessful in doing so but in the process attained heaven.

When the brilliant King Dilipa heard the stories of his grandfathers, he was overtaken by grief and was thinking about ways to bring the River Ganga onto the earth and ways to carry out the funeral rites of his ancestors. He was constantly engaged in these thoughts.

King Dilipa was blessed with a highly virtuous son, Bhagiratha, who was free from all malice. Dilipa ruled the kingdom in the same virtuous ways as his father. King Dilipa then performed the coronation of his son Bhagiratha. King Dilipa left for forest and underwent severe penances to bring Ganga to earth, just like his father. But although trying with his power, he could not bring about what he so much wished. In due course of time, he passed away.

King Bhagiratha's Determination

King Bhagiratha was a great King and a great warrior. He was able to delight every soul of his country. Under him, the kingdom was flourishing, and people were extremely happy.

When the King learned that his forefathers had met their ends by the wrath of Sage Kapila and their souls were still not able to reach heaven, he had sunken into deep sorrow. With deep heart, the King handed over the reigns of his kingdom to the council of ministers and went to the Himalayas to worship Ganga.

With his arms uplifted, partaking food once a month, with his senses controlled, he carried out deep yogic penance. After a long duration of penance, pleased with Bhagiratha's determination, Devi Ganga, assuming the material form, manifested to him in her divine form.

Ganga then said, *"O great King, what do you desire of me? What must I give you? Tell me, I shall do what you wish for, I am pleased with your penance."* On hearing these words of the daughter of Himalaya, the King bowed to her with respect and said, *"O great river! My forefather, King Sagara's sixty thousand sons, were reduced to ashes by the great Sage Kapila. They will be able to attain salvation only through the touch of your waters. For this, I beg you to flow down to earth."*

Devi Ganga, very pleased with the King, said, *"O King, I am ready to bestow your wish, but when falling from the sky to earth, the earth will not be able to sustain the force of my fall. In all the worlds, there is none other than the Mighty Lord Shiva, the Neelakanta, the wielder of Trishul (trident), who can sustain this force. He will be able to sustain force on his matted hairs, and then I can descend onto earth and thereby fulfil your wish. Hence, you need to obtain his favour through severe austerities."*

King Bhagiratha then stood on his toes and carried out severe penance for Lord Shiva. Within a short period of time, the omnipresent Lord Shiva was pleased and appeared before King Bhagiratha. Granting the prayers of the King, Lord Shiva then said, *"O best of men, I am pleased with your devotion, I shall hold Ganga on my head to reduce the force of her descent. I shall do as you wish."*

The Descent of Goddess Ganga

Hearing the words of the Supreme God, the King bowed to Him and directed his thoughts towards Devi Ganga. Thus, on being invited by the King, Goddess Ganga, in the form of the delightful river of pure water, started to fall with mighty force from heaven. To visualise this magnificent sight, all Devatas, Gandharvas, great Sages, Yakshas, etc assembled there as spectators. As she was falling with a rage of whirlpools, various fishes were also present. While descending, Lord Shiva took her into the depths of his matted locks of hair.

Lord Shiva then released the Ganga onto the earth. From the sky to Lord Shiva's head and then to earth, Ganga flowed with a roaring sound. White foams of water were scattered everywhere, like a flock of swans spread in the sky. Ganga was now flowing slower but wider, twisting and turning through the valleys high and low, waves rising up and down, cleaning off all impurities. She then told King Bhagiratha, *"O great King, show me the path that I must take. For your sake, I have descended onto the earth."* Having heard these words, the King, mounting on his divine chariot, moved forward, and Ganga followed. Behind Ganga, all the

ॐ

Devatas, Sages, Daityas, Nagas, and Gandharvas followed them with utmost joy. King Bhagiratha directed her course towards the spot where the mighty sons of King Sagara were burnt. Accompanied by King Bhagiratha, she reached the sea, the abode of Varuna. People rejoiced at the sight of the shining water and were happy to have a dip in the Ganga and rejuvenate themselves.

The holy water of Ganga flooded the heaps of ashes of the sons of King Sagara and purged off their sins, and they were thus liberated and ascended to heaven. Lord Brahma then appeared before King Bhagiratha and said, *"O King, sixty thousand sons of illustrious King Sagara have been liberated and gone to heaven. This Ganga will be your eldest daughter and will also be known as Bhagirathi. As she now also flows in the three worlds, she will also be called Tripathaga."*

King Bhagiratha Returns

The King having performed the rites for his ancestor's liberation. His desire thus being fulfilled, he returned to his kingdom and continued serving his kingdom in most virtuous way.

The son of Bhagiratha was Shruta and from Shruta, Nabhaga was born. Nabhaga had a son named Ambarisha. Ambarisha was the father of Sindhudvipa. Sindhudvipa had a son named Ayutayu.

Chapter 13

King Rituparna:
Story of Nala – Damayanti

King Rituparna

King Ayutayu, who ruled the kingdom of Ayodhya, crowned his son Rituparna as the new King. King Rituparna was a master of archery and other deadly weapons. He was also well-versed in the game of dice, which was famous during that period. King Rituparna was not only a mighty warrior but also a very generous King. He was a staunch devotee of Lord Vishnu.

The Divine Love of Nala and Damayanti

In the kingdom of Nishadha, there was a King named Nala, who was the son of Virasena. Nala was an accomplished king, and his glory resembled the glory of the sun. He was strong, most handsome, well-versed in knowledge of horses. He was respectful of Brahmins, well-versed in Vedas, truthful and a master of a mighty army. He was loved by all the men and women of his kingdom.

During the same period, there was another valiant King named Bhima, who ruled the kingdom of Vidarbha. He was a King of great power, heroic, possessed of every virtue. But he was

ॐ

---

childless and with intent of having offsprings, performed great austerities. Once, a Brahmarishi named Damana arrived at his palace. King Bhima, along with his queen, gave a great respectful reception. Sage Damana was pleased with the couple and granted them a boon. As a result of the boon, they soon had a daughter, Damayanti and three sons of great fame – Dama, Danta, and Damana. As she grew, Princess Damayanti turned out to be the most beautiful lady with faultless features. Decked with every ornament, she became celebrated all around the world for her beauty and goodness.

As fate would have, the people used to praise Damayanti in front of Nala and about Nala to Damayanti. On hearing each other's virtues regularly, there grew an attachment towards one another, even though they hadn't seen each other. As days passed, the mental attachment began to grow in strength. Nala began to spend more time thinking about Damayanti in the solitude of the garden.

One day, while sitting in his garden, lost in the thoughts of Damayanti, he saw several swans wandering there. He caught hold of one of them, but to his surprise, the swan in a human voice told him, *"O King of Nishadha, please don't kill me. I will speak before Damayanti about you in such a way that she will fall in love with you."* The king then let the swan loose, and it flew away to the kingdom of Vidarbha.

The swan then approached Princess Damayanti and started praising Nala's beauty and his virtues. The swan also told her that there is no man equal to him in beauty. Damayanti then told the swan that it should go back to Nala and praise about her to Nala in the same way. The swan then followed Damayanti's orders.

Damayanti's Swayamvara

Hearing the words of the beautiful swan, the princess, too, remained lost in thoughts always. Lost in love, she lost her hunger and sleep. In due course of time, she became pale, weak, and lost all inclination towards materialistic enjoyment. Seeing the plight of her daughter, King Bhima became worried. He felt that time had arrived for her marriage. So, he began the arrangements for her swayamvara and started inviting kings and princes from far and wide. Hearing about Damayanti's swayamvara, all the kings came to Vidarbha. King Bhima honoured each one of the guests and gave them their quarters.

Meanwhile, Sage Narada visited Indra in heaven and gave the news of what was going on around the world to him. On enquiring about the Kshatriya heroes, Sage Narada told Indra about the daughter of the King of Vidarbha, Damayanti and described her unmatched beauty to the Devatas. He then informed them about the ongoing Swayamvara, where all the heroes of earth had gathered. Hearing this, all the Devatas also decided to participate in the Swayamvara, and so did the most generous King of Nishadha, Nala.

When the Devatas were going for the swayamvara, they saw the most handsome, Nala, who was shining bright like the glorious sun. Seeing him, The Devatas quit their wish to marry Damayanti, but to test him, they approached Nala and told him, *"O foremost ruler of Nishadha, kindly help us and be our messenger."* Nala, hearing the words of Devatas, replied, *"I will do as you say."* The Indra then spoke, *"I am Indra, he is Agni, he is Varuna, and he is Yama. Kindly inform Damayanti that we are coming for the swayamvara, and we desire to obtain her. So, she should choose one of us."*

Nala then humbly told them that he himself had come full of love for Damayanti and desired to obtain her as a wife. Further, he said in such a situation, how can he be the messenger of others with the same cause? The Devatas then reminded him that he had promised to do so and could not back out. Nala then told that palace of Damayanti is completely guarded, and no one would allow to enter it. Indra then told him that he would be able to enter by their grace.

Nala thereupon arrived at the palace of Damayanti and saw her surrounded by her maids. Nala was awe-struck when he saw Damayanti blazing in her beauty. Seeing her, his love for her only increased. Seeing Nala, Damayanti, struck in amazement, smiling, enquired about his whereabouts and the reason for his coming there. Nala then replied, *"My name is Nala, and I came here as a messenger of Indra, Agni, Varuna and Yama, and they desire to have you as theirs. O beautiful lady, do choose one of them."*

Damayanti then replied, *"Me and whatever of mine is all yours. My love is only for you, and I would like to marry you. I had called this swayamvara only to be married to you. If you don't accept me as your wife, I will lay down my life by poison or fire."* Nala then asked her, *"When the Devatas themselves would like to marry you, why me? Who is not equal to them? Displeasing the Devatas could lead to your end. Besides being with Devatas, you will be able to enjoy eternal happiness."*

Damayanti then said that he had already chosen him (Nala) as her husband. Nala then said he is presently there as a messenger of the Devatas, and he must follow the rules of a messenger, and she must find a way to righteously consider him as her husband. Damayanti then said, *"O great among men, I have found a blameless way. Tomorrow at the ceremony, you will be present at the hall, and I will choose you as my husband in the presence of the Devatas, and no one will blame you.*" Nala then returned to the Devatas and narrated the entire episode.

At the auspicious hour of the ceremony, King Bhima summoned all the kings and princes to the hall for the swayamvara. All the Devatas, assuming the form of Nala, were also present there along with Nala. All of them had a garland of fragrant flowers in their hand and waited for Damayanti. Then, Damayanti, with a beautiful face and gorgeous eyes, entered the hall and glanced at the great warriors present there. Her eyes were looking for the one for the one whom she had given her heart to.

Damayanti then saw five people who looked alike in appearance. They looked like Nala, and Bhima's daughter was unable to distinguish the real Nala among them. She was in total confusion and scared. With fear in mind, Damayanti then said to all the five, *"I am already in love with King Nala and in my mind, I have already accepted him as my husband. So, kindly reveal yourself and guide me to the real King Nala. I had also carried out deep penance to obtain him. Hey Devatas, please reveal him to me."* Seeing Damayanti's true love, her determination and affection for Nala, the Devatas revealed themselves to Damayanti. Damayanti then put the garland on to Nala and accepted him as her husband. Nala then said, *"O blessed one, in the presence of the celestial ones, you have chosen this mortal one. For this, I will always be at your side, fulfilling your wishes; know me as your husband. I pledge this to you."*

The couple got married in front of the holy fire and the Devatas, and they were pleased to be one. On completion of the ceremony, the Devatas gave them boons. Indra told him that he should be able to behold his godship in sacrifices and that he should attain blessed legions. Agni gave him a boon that he would appear before him whenever he desired, and his region would be as bright as Agni himself. Yama blessed him by saying that the food prepared in his kitchen would be of supreme taste and that he would always remain virtuous. Varuna also gave him a boon that he would be present whenever Nala wanted water, and his garland flowers would remain fragrant for eternity. Nala and Damayanti stayed at Bhima's residence for a few more days as per tradition and, after that, left for Nishadha.

The beautiful couple, Nala and Damayanti lived happily. Soon they were blessed with a son who was named Indrasen and daughter named Indrasena. Thus, the King Nala ruled the kingdom abounding in wealth by performing sacrifices and living in the company of his wife.

The Wrath of Kalipurush

Meanwhile, while the Devatas were returning from the swayamvara of Damayanti, they met Kali (Kalipurush of Kaliyug), who was also on the way to attend the same function. Indra then said that Damayanti's swayamvara was already over, and she chose Nala as her husband. Kali was furious as she had chosen a mortal being over the celestial. Devatas told him that Nala was very virtuous, and it was with their (Devatas) consent that the marriage took place. Kali then said to himself, *"I am unable to control my anger, and I will enter Nala's body and make him lose his kingdom by making him play dice and thereby pay the price for what has happened."*

Kali reached place Nala's residence and observed him daily. As Nala was a very virtuous person, Kali could not enter his body, so he kept waiting for an opportunity to enter Nala's body. After twelve years, one day, Nala forgot to wash his feet before the prayers, and Kali got his opportunity. Having possessed Nala, he appeared before Pushkara and invited him to play a game of dice.

Nala, being possessed by Kali, started to lose all his wealth, his chariot, all his clothing, etc., as the game went on. Even though all the people and councillors around him tried to stop him from playing the game, nothing worked. The citizens wanted to meet the King for their daily problems or other duties, but the King, ignoring them, continued with the game. Seeing the plight of her husband, Damayanti's eyes were filled with tears. Struck with grief and fear, the queen tried to stop the King, but in vain.

Sensing the worst, the Queen sent her son and daughter to Kundipur and left the kids in the care of her brothers through Nala's charioteer, Varshneya. After leaving the kids with King Bhima, Varshneya entered the kingdom of Ayodhya and entered into the service of King Rituparna.

Meanwhile, King Nala lost everything, including his kingdom, to Pushkara and was left only with his wife Damayanti. When Pushkara asked to put Damayanti at stake, the virtuous king's heart burst with rage but remained silent. He renounced all his wealth and his robes and then, along with Damayanti in her single piece of cloth, left the city. Pushkara then announced to the citizens that he, who helped Nala, would be doomed. Hence, the people could show no hospitality towards them, and the couple started wandering without food and shelter. Nala then kept telling Damayanti to return to her father, to which Damayanti said that she would go to her house only if Nala accompanied her and stayed with her there. She also assured Nala that King Bhima would honour them both and they could live happily.

Wandering through the woods, they reached a shelter shed and Damayanti, who was tired, soon fell asleep. Distraught Nala, influenced by Kali, thought of deserting her, and hoped she would reach her parents and live happily. Nala prayed to Devatas to protect his wife, whom he was deserting.

Under the influence of Kali, Nala would go out but would return to his wife again, drawn by love. Finally, under the Kali effect, the king, tearing half her clothes for himself, departed in sorrow, leaving her alone.

When Damayanti woke up, she couldn't find her husband, so she started crying and calling him. She started wandering through the forest in search of her husband. In the forest, she was attacked by a python but was saved by a hunter. But the hunter tried to attack her, she then cursed him and was burnt to death by the forest fire that erupted. She then travelled further, where she met Rishis, who comforted her. She then met some merchant travellers who were willing to take her to the kingdom of Chedis. But as fate would have it, the travellers were crushed by a herd of wild elephants. After a lot of adventures and struggles, she finally reached the kingdom of Chedi and met Queen Bhanumati. She stayed there on one condition: that she would not be approached by any males and would be treated with respect. Damayanti then continued to reside there without anxiety of any kind, for all her wishes were duly gratified.

Nala meet King Rituparna

After deserting the queen Damayanti, Nala when travelling in forest, saw huge blaze of fire in the forest and heard a noise, *"O the great Nala, please help me."* Nala then replied, *"Don't fear."* Saying this he entered the fire and rescued the Naga king, Karkotaka. The Naga King said that he was cursed by Sage Narada for deceiving him and was told that he would be lying there, unable to move until saved by King Nala.

Nala then moved the Naga out of the region of fire and set him free. Naga then told Nala to count his steps and walk. He would provide him with something which would serve as a boon. Nala, as soon as he counted to ten, the Naga bit him. Nala turned into an ugly dwarf. The Naga then said, *"O King Nala, my poison in your body will affect the Kali who is inside you, he will be suffering inside you till he leaves your body. You don't deserve to be deceived and troubled, I did this to save you from him. Because of this, you will never be affected by any curse or poison from any fanged animals, and you will always be victorious in war. You may now change your name to Bahuka and introduce yourself to King Rituparna of the Ikshvaku dynasty, who is an expert in the game of dice, as a charioteer. When you want to regain your original form, you may wear this cloth and remember me."* The Naga King, who gave him the cloth, left.

After ten days of travelling, King Nala reached the kingdom of King Rituparna. On meeting the King, Nala introduced himself, saying, *"I am Bahuka, and there is no one better than me at managing horses. I am in a financial crisis. You may also seek my counsel in any matters of difficulty and an excellent cook. I can also carry out any difficult art. I beg you to keep me with you."* Hearing this, King Rituparna said that he had always wanted someone to train his horse so that he could reach any destination quickly. Bahuka was appointed as the chief of the stables in the company of Varshney and Jivala.

Nala spent his days in disguise of Bahuka, in the kingdom of Rituparna, lost in thoughts of his beloved wife, Damayanti. He used to weep thinking of Damayanti, and once, when asked by Jivala, he told her that he had left her wife in the forest, and he had torn her half clothes for himself and had them there.

Damayanti's Return to Vidarbha

King Bhima on hearing about Nala Damayanti's kingdom of Nishadha being taken over by Pushkara. On learning that his daughter and son-in-law had gone to the forest, the king announced that anyone who finds them and brings them home will be rewarded handsomely. On hearing this announcement, everyone started searching for them in all directions. Then, one day, a Brahmana named Sudeva saw the princess of Vidarbha seated with Sunanda in the palace of Chedis. Sudeva could recognise the incomparable beauty, though slightly diminished due to lack of ornaments. Devoid of comforts and luxuries, separated from loved ones and friends, she lived in distress, supported by the hope of beholding her beloved husband one day. Without the husband by her side, though beautiful, she was not shining.

Sudeva then told Damayanti, *"O princess of Vidarbha, I am Sudeva, a friend of your brother. I came here by the wish of your father. Your father, mother, brothers and their sons and daughters are well and living in peace. All the Brahmanas have been sent out in search of you and your husband."* Damayanti recognised Sudeva and then started crying. Seeing this, Sunanda informed the queen-mother, and she came out and asked Sudeva about who Damayanti was. Sudeva then related the story of Damayanti to her. On hearing this, the Queen-mother said, *"O beautiful girl, your mother and I are the daughters of Swami Mahamanar of Dasharna. And I have seen you when you were a kid; you were born in the kingdom of Dasharna."*

Damayanti was glad and said, *"Even though you didn't know me, you had taken great care of me. I know now that you know me, you will take care of me more than ever. But please allow me to go to my mother's as I have been travelling a lot. My kids have been away, and I am eagerly waiting to meet them. Kindly make arrangements for my return."* With the permission of the King of Chedi, Damayanti was given a grand send-off, escorted by a large troop, and received an abundance of food and water.

ॐ

In a few days, Damayanti reached Vidarbha and met her parents, relatives, and friends. She was welcomed, and she respected all Brahmanas. In the night, when she was at her father's palace, she told her mother that if they wanted to see her alive, they should continue the search for her husband, Nala. Thereafter, King Bhima ordered the search for Nala. Damayanti told the Brahmanas who were to go searching to say these words, *"O beloved gambler, where have you gone tearing half my cloth, deserting the dear and devoted wife in the forest? The wife is always to be protected and maintained by the husband. Why, then, has someone as good as you, possessed of fame and wisdom, been so unkind."* Thus instructed the Brahmanas to set out in all directions.

Damayanti's Swayamvara

One day, a Brahmana named Panaarda returned from Ayodhya and told Damayanti, *"When I narrated the words said by you in the hall of King Rituparna, no one said anything, neither the king nor anyone from the crowd. Then, when I was about to leave, a charioteer named Bahuka, who was short and dark, approached me in loneliness and said that virtuous women, when in distress, protect themselves and live a virtuous life; there is no doubt about it. Such women don't get angry, whether treated well or ill-treated, because their husband was deprived of kingdom or wealth and was lost in grief and hunger, overwhelmed with calamity. He drives the chariot very fast and is an excellent cook. Hearing these words, I came running to you."*

Hearing this, Damayanti rewarded the Brahmana and sent Brahmana Sudeva to Ayodhya to give a message to King Rituparna that Damayanti was holding another swayamvara, and all kings and princes were invited. On hearing this, King Rituparna told

ॐ

Bahuka that he wished to attend the swayamvara and that he should reach Vidarbha in a day. Nala thought that Damayanti must have taken this decision in the plight of grief. At the orders of the King, Bahuka selected the best horse and, along with charioteer Varshney and King Rituparna, drove the chariot with the speed of the wind. Varshney doubted that the skills of Bahuka were like Nala's. During the journey, Nala requested the King to teach him the secrets of the game of dice.

At that moment, Kali, who was suffering inside the body of Nala, came out. He was in dire strait. Nala was about to curse him, but Kali said he was already suffering heavily inside Nala's body and said, *"If you don't curse me, any person who recites your valour story will never be harmed by me."* After Nala had gone, Kali returned to his abode. Nala has not returned to his original form yet.

The chariot reached the kingdom of Bhima, but Rituparna didn't see any arrangements of swayamvara. Rituparna then said he came there to pay a visit to the King of Vidarbha; though confused, King Bhima told him to take a rest. Meanwhile, Damayanti heard the chariot speeding to the palace but could not see Nala. But she could feel his presence.

Damayanti then sent Koshiyani, her maid, to find out about Bahuka. Initially, she could not find out if Bahuka was Nala, so Damayanti again sent her to keep a close eye on what and how Bahuka was doing his work and told her when he asked for fire or water, don't give him. Koshiyani did as instructed. Koshiyani then returned and told Damayanti that his work was very precise and that he carried out all work with utmost purity. Entering any space with low head space, he never had to bend down. Even when there was no water in the pot, he was able to wash the food items in water. He could light a fire with a handful of grass.

Damayanti then told Koshiyani to bring some food prepared by Bahuka. On tasting it, Damayanti confirmed Bahuka was Nala himself. Damayanti then cried aloud in grief and sent her children in front of Nala. Nala, upon seeing his children, cried out loudly and embraced them. Nala, coming back to his senses, again left the children and told Koshiyani that they were like his children, so remembering them, he shed tears. He told Koshiyani not to visit him frequently, as he was a guest of the kingdom, and people would think wrong about them.

Koshiyani then went back to Damayanti and narrated the entire thing. Damayanti was sure that Bahuka was Nala himself, so she went to her mother and told her doubts and asked her to arrange a meeting with Bahuka, with or without the permission of her father. King Bhima gave them permission, and Bahuka was brought to the residence.

Re-union of Nala and Damayanti

Seeing Damayanti in a piece of red cloth covered in dust and dirt, Nala, who was in the form of Bahuka, was overwhelmed with grief and was in tears. Damayanti then asked Bahuka, *"O Bahuka, have you ever seen a virtuous person, other than Nala, who would desert his dear wife who was sleeping in the forest? First, during swayamvara, in front of fire and Devatas, he accepts me, marries me, promises to be there for me always, has children with me, and then deserts me."*

While Damayanti was saying this, tears began to flow from Nala's reddish eyes, and he then said, *"Neither the loss of my kingdom nor desertion of you was my act. Kali was living inside me like a fire inside the fire. The sinful Kali has now left me, and I have come here. It is only for you that I have come and no other purpose. How can a lady leave a loving husband and marry another?"*

Hearing Nala's words, Damayanti was terrified and, with palms joined, replied, *"You shouldn't doubt my character, as I had chosen you over the celestial Devatas during the swayamvara. After sending the Brahmins everywhere in search of you, Brahmin Pranaarda bought me information. Based on this, we had sent Sudeva to send a message to King Rituparna of the swayamvara, which was supposed to happen the next day. I know there is no one in this world except you who could reach such a long distance in one day. May all witnessing air take my life if I have committed the sin."*

King Nala, the destroyer of enemies, cast away all his doubts, remembering the Naga King, wore the garment given to him and thus regained his original form. Seeing her lord in real form, Damayanti embraced him and wept aloud. Nala also embraced her and the kids. The next day, King Rituparna also heard that Nala and Damayanti were united. He asked Nala for forgiveness for anything wrong said or done to him during his stay in Ayodhya.

Nala then replied, *"O great King, you have never done anything wrong to me, and I bear no anger towards you. You have always fulfilled all my wishes there, and I was always happy there."*

Saying this, Nala taught him the Ashwavigyan, the science of horse, and in return, King Rituparna taught him the secrets of the game of dice. After this, along with the other chariot, the great king Rituparna returned to his kingdom.

Nala Defeats Pushkara

After staying in Vidarbha for a few days, Nala, with a small troop, returned to Nishadha and told Pushkara, *"Hey Pushkara, I have gained some wealth. Let's again play a game of dice. Along with wealth, I am willing to put my wife and family on the line. In return, you must put the entire kingdom. If you agree to this, we play the game, or you must fight a war with me."* Pushkara was ready for the game of dice as he had his eyes on the ever-so-beautiful Damayanti. Hearing this, Nala was angry and wanted to cut Pushkara's head off but agreed to play one game of dice. In the game, Nala won, and Pushkara, who had put his entire kingdom, wealth, and his life at stake, lost.

Nala then told Pushkara, *"Now the entire kingdom is back under my control, and you will never ever lay your eyes on my Damayanti. You and your family will be my slave. Previously, you had won because of Kali, who was inside me."* Nala then again told his Pushkara, *"I give you back your wealth and family. Go back to your kingdom, and I will always consider you my brother. Lead a good, long life."* Saying this, Nala sent Pushkara off to his kingdom. Pushkara, overwhelmed with respect for King Nala, left for his capital.

Seeing Nala back as their king, the citizens of his kingdom were very pleased. Thereafter, Nala went to Vidarbha to bring back his wife, Damayanti and the kids. Thereafter, they lived happily and ruled the kingdom in the most virtuous way. The story of Nala Damayanti is not part of the Ikshvaku Dynasty, but this history of the Naga Karkotaka, of Damayanti, of Nala and of that royal sage Rituparna when listened to, can destroy the evil influence of Kali inside one.

King Rituparna and His Progeny

King Rituparna was succeeded by his son, Sarvakarma. Sarvakarma had a son named Sudaasa. Saudasa, also known as Mitrasaha, was the son of Sudaasa. Saudaasa married Madayanti and had carried a son for seven years in her womb. Madayati then, using a sharp stone, divided her womb, and a son was born. The son was named Ashmak.

Ashmak then gave birth to a son named Mulak. When Parashuram had attacked all Kshatriyas around the world, then Mulak was saved by a number of women. Hence, he was named Narikavacha. Mulak's son was Dasaratha, his son was Ilivile, and Vishvasaha was born from him.

Chapter 14

King Dilipa: The Invinscible King

The Great King Dilipa

The ruler of Ayodhya, King Vishvasaha, had a son who was named Dilipa. Dilipa was the disciple of Guru Vasishta, and he was a great student. He mastered the art of warfare, diplomacy and state administration. After King Vishvasaha, Dilipa was crowned as the king of Ayodhya. He was a mighty warrior, a virtuous and generous king. There was no one equal in him in valour and was the sovereign ruler of the world. He performed numerous yajnas and hence was also known as Khatvanga.

King Dilipa Meets Sage Vasishta

The King, the best among men, was married to the daughter of King Magadha, Sudakhshina. Even after a long time, they were not blessed with a child. This worried the sovereign king, who had accomplished everything, carried out several austerities and worshipped the Lord.

The King one day handed over the reign of the kingdom to his councillors, and along with his wife, he left for the forest to meet Sage Vasishta. On entering the hermitage, they saw Sage was performing rites and his wife Arundhati was beside him. On completion of the rites, the King touched the feet of Sage while the queen took the blessings of Devi Arundhati and took their blessing. The adorable Sage honoured the guests with respectful offerings and enquired about the purpose of their visit.

The King told the Sage, *"O Brahmana, with a desire to go to heaven, I have abandoned my kingdom and come to your hermitage to practice penance. Kings born in the Ikshvaku family have entrusted their kingdom to their sons, but when I die, whom will I pass my kingdom to without a child? Kindly tell me the defect due to which a son was not born to me."* Having heard the King, Sage closed his eyes and went into deep meditation. When he opened his eyes, he told the King replied, *"O King, once when you had gone to meet Indra, on your way back, eager to meet your queen, you did not notice the divine desire-yielding cow, Kamdhenu, and thereby, disrespected her. In anger, she cursed you that you will not have a son born to you until you serve her progeny. So, you and your wife must serve and worship her granddaughter, cow Nandini, and her calf. Only then will you be blessed with a son. You must serve her by going with her to the forest and protecting her, while the queen will serve her when she returns to the hermitage. This is to be done for a period of twenty-one days."*

Testing the King

In the morning, the queen worshipped the cow and the calf. After worship, the King would take her to the forest by the King. He would eat his food only after the cow ate grass. He drank water only after she drank; he sat under the shade only after the cow sat. The King thus served the divine cow by offering her soft grass, driving away flies and scratching her body. The Queen, after the cow returned to the hermitage, stood before her with palms joined and duly worshipping her. Thus, twenty days passed, with the queen and king serving her diligently.

One day, the cow entered a cave in the Himalayas while grazing the grass. The King appreciated the beauty of the Himalayan peaks when suddenly, a lion appeared from nowhere and caught hold of the cow. The cow started crying piteously. The King then took out an arrow, fixed it on the bow, and aimed at the lion but could not discharge the arrow. The Lion, to his amazement, spoke to the King in a human voice, *"I know you as Dilipa of the Ikshvaku race, and I am Lord Shiva's attendant, Kumbhodara. I am protected by Devi Parvati. Once, the soft bark of this tree was badly torn by the wild elephants. Taking pity, Devi turned me into a lion to protect it and told me to eat whichever animal would come here."*

Hearing this the King though paralysed, replied, *"I pay my respect to Lord Shiva and Devi Parvati. This cow, by name Nandini, belongs to Sage Vasishta and I am here to serve and protect her. I am aware that It is not possible to forcibly her release from you, O server of Shiva and I cannot go back to Sage without the cow. Instead of the cow, you may have me as your meal."*

Saying, the King sat down submissively, expecting to be pounced upon by the lion. Instead, flowers dropped from the sky, and a divine voice was heard. King opened his eyes, and so did no lion. Nandini then told King, *"Everything that you saw here was a maya, an illusion created by me to test you. I am pleased to say you passed the test"*.

Birth of Raghu

Nandini further said, *"O King, by Sage's power, even Yama cannot touch me, then what other animals can do to me. I pleased with your devotion, and you may ask for a boon."* The King then made a request to bless the Queen Sudakhshina for the continuity of his family with a son.

Nandini then said, *"Make a cup of leaves drink to your satisfaction my milk, and when you reach the hermitage, after an order from Sage, drink the remaining milk, and then you will have a son who will be mighty and bring glory to your race."* The King then replied that he would take the milk after the young calf had fed itself and Sage's rites were complete with milk. Nandini was pleased, and they returned to the hermitage.

The King narrated the entire episode to Sage Vasishta and the Queen. After the calf had its feed and with the permission of Sage, the King and Queen drank the milk of the cow. Next day after completion of all rituals and service to the cow, returned to their Kingdom. After a few months, the queen became pregnant and soon gave birth to a son named Raghu.

King Dilipa Attains Moksha

Once a huge battle broke out between the Asuras and Devatas. Asuras were overwhelming in the war, so they sought the help of the mighty King Dilipa. Being entreated by Devatas, the invincible king destroyed many asuras. Being pleased with the King, the Devatas asked him to request a boon of his choice.

The King told them, *"The battle in which I participle alongside you was like yajna to me. I am happy to have been able to provide you with my service. This is a boon in itself."* The Devatas then compelled him to ask for some boon. The King then said, *"If you press me to accept a boon, tell me the duration of my life left."* The Devatas then replied, *"O King, your life is almost over. You are left with only one muhurat (a few minutes)."* Hearing this, the King came down as quickly as possible in the chariot gifted by Devatas.

Having reached the earth, he prayed to the Supreme Vishnu and said, *"My soul has never been dearer to me than the*

Brahmins; if I have never deviated from my duties if I have never differentiated between any men, Devatas, animals, birds, or trees from the imperishable one, then may I attain the Supreme Being, whom I meditate."

The King thus gave up attachment to the Gunas – rajas and tamas, through deep devotion and had his mind firmly fixed on the very root of everything that exists, the Supreme Truth. Having thus determined by his intellect, discarding the ignorance and false attachment to his body, The King's soul attained the Supreme Brahman, the Absolute Truth.

The Saptarishis said the following about the King: *"There shall be no King like Khatvanga. He came from heaven, dwelt on earth for a muhurat, and became united with Lord of all worlds by means of the knowledge of Absolute Truth."*

Chapter 15

King Raghu and King Aja: The Glorious Kings

Reign of King Raghu

King Dilipa's kingdom was inherited by Raghu, his son. He was the mighty king of Ayodhya, and the dynasty further came to be known as Raghuvansham. He ruled his kingdom in virtuous ways as per Sage Vashishta. He was involved in the welfare of varnas of the society. The varnas were classified as Brahmins (priests, teachers, intellectuals), Kshatriyas (Kings, warriors, administrators), Vaishyas (traders, merchants, farmers) and Shudra (artisans, labourers, etc). He used to win over the enemies in peaceful manners or by diplomatic tactics. He was a skilled warrior and is known for his great chariot driving abilities.

King had expanded his territories in all directions. First, he expanded his territory to the eastern coast, defeating Suhmas and Vangas. Crossing the river, he conquers the country of Kalinga. He then marched towards the south and subdued the Pandya Kings. Across the Sindhu River, he subdued the Hunas and Kambhojas. Across the Himalayas, he brings the Utsavamketas under his rule.

King Raghu and Brahmin Kautsa

King Raghu was a generous king; it was said that no one returned empty-handed from his palace. At the instruction from Sage

Vashishta, King Raghu performed the Vishvajit yajna and donated all his wealth. After completion of the yajna, a Brahmin by the name of Kautsa approached the King and asked for financial help of fourteen crore gold coins. On enquiry, Kautsa narrated his story: –

"On completion of my education, I asked my Guru Vartanu what I should give him as my Guru-Dakshina, but My Guru said he didn't need anything, and he was satisfied in having me as his disciple and imparting me the knowledge. But I was not satisfied with the answer, so I insisted on Guru-Dakshina. Annoyed with me, Sage Vartantu said he had given me fourteen vidyas, so in return, I must give him fourteen crore gold coins. So, I came here requesting your assistance."

The King, having completed the yajna and his treasure emptied, was left with no wealth. So, he decided to attack Kubera, the god of wealth. But before he could attack, understanding the King's intention, Kubera showered the gold coins from the sky at the onset of dawn. The King collected the gold coins and gave them to Kautsa. Kautsa, being Brahmin, told them he would need only the fourteen thousand coins. The rest of the coins were distributed among the citizens of Ayodhya.

Pleased with the generosity of the king, Kuatsa and Sage Vartantu blessed the great King to beget a son who would inherit his empire and be a great ruler.

Story of Aja and Indumati

One day, in the early Brahma hours, the Queen of Ayodhya gave birth to a son and was named Aja. As Prince Aja grew older, he showed the characters and the physique just like his father. One day, the King of Vidarbha, Bhoja, sent an invitation to Prince Aja for the swayamvara of his sister Indumati. As the Prince, too, had reached his marriageable age, King Raghu sent him along with his army to Vidarbha for the swayamvara.

King Bhoja himself went to welcome Prince Aja as he arrived at the outskirts of the city of Kundinapur, the capital of Vidarbha. As Prince Aja entered the palace, he was welcomed by the King's council of ministers as he made his way to the royal guest room.

The day of Swayamvara finally arrived. Prince Aja completed his morning rituals and, dressed in his majestic outfit, proceeded to the assembly hall where all other Kings had gathered. Amidst those Kings, Prince Aja, Raghu's son, shone with majestic lustre. Seeing him, all the other kings felt down in confidence of winning the hands of Princess Indumati.

As the sounds of auspicious musical instruments filled the air, a palanquin carried by bearers arrived and was placed in the middle of the rows of daises where Kings were seated. From the palanquin came out the most gorgeous-looking princess, Indumati. Seeing the princess, all the kings present there were astonished at her beauty, and their eyes were glued to her. Indumati's attendant introduced her to the kings one by one as they passed each one of them.

On reaching the seat of King Raghu's son, Indumati's eyes and heart were fixed on him. She was unwilling to move forward. The princess placed the garland of auspicious flowers around the neck of the prince and thereby chose him as her husband. King Bhoja then arranged the couple's marriage in a grand style. On completion of the marriage ceremony, the prince and his wife returned to the kingdom of Ayodhya. On his way back, some of the kings who could not obtain the princess in marriage attacked Prince Aja. The valiant Prince then defeated them and sent them back. Raghu, who had the details of his son's deeds, welcomed him and his praiseworthy wife. The King has decided that it is time for him to hand over the reign of the kingdom to his son.

King Raghu's Retirement

Sage Vashishta conducted the coronation of Prince Aja using the waters brought from all sacred rivers. King Aja became invincible by his enemies. The citizens of his kingdom considered Prince Aja as incarnation of their favourite King Raghu himself, as he had not only inherited his royal grace but also the traits of his character.

Seeing his son established among his people, King Raghu decided to retire to the forest where he would leave the materialistic pleasures of the world and obtain oneness with the Supreme like his ancestors. King Raghu sought the help of the Sage to concentrate and guide him to attain Moksha. The retired King Raghu sat on the grass to practice concentration and bring the vital senses under his control.

Meanwhile, King Aja, along with his efficient council of ministers, continued to bring under his control land which had not yet been conquered. The King was now in complete control of his kingdom and had been taking care of the needs of the people of the city in the best possible ways.

Demise of Indumati

Queen Indumati delivered a valiant son named Dasharatha. He was known for his fame in all ten quarters of the world.

One day, when King Aja was strolling in the Nandana garden. It was the same time when Sage Narada was on his journey through the sky. Suddenly, a heavy wind blew, and the garland of celestial flowers on his musical instrument flew off and fell on the Queen Indumati. The Queen suddenly collapsed and went into an eternal sleep. As she was falling, she fell on the King, who became unconscious. The King regained consciousness after a few moments, but by then, the queen had passed away. The King, who was in extreme love with his wife, held her in his lap and started crying out aloud, *"Today all my courage has disappeared, my desire for enjoyment has come to a halt, the season is without pleasure, I am quite alone. You were my wife, my councillor, my companion, everything that I am. Now, my life has been snatched by your ruthless death. Without you, my desire to live has ceased."*

After ten days, the funeral ceremony of Indumati, of whom only the virtues survived, was completed by the moaning King Aja. The family priest Vashishta, though his immense power of his austerities understood the story of the King's grief. He conveyed the story of Indumati to the mourning King.

Story of Indumati

Seeing the plight of King Aja, Sage Narada came down and narrated the story of Indumati to him. It was the period when Devata King Indra was growing apprehensive about the penance that was being performed by Maharishi Trinabindu. Harini was an Apsara in the court of Indra, and she was superlative in her beauty. Indra approached her and instructed her to interrupt Maharishi Trinabindu's penance using her skills.

Apsara Harini sincerely followed the task given by her King, Indra and was successful in obstructing the Maharishi's penance. Angered by this, Maharishi cursed her to be born as a mortal woman in the mortal world (earth). Apsara Harini then pleaded to Maharishi and rendered a sincere apology. She told him that it was not her personal intention to distract him, and she had just obeyed Indra's command. Maharishi then said the curse cannot be reversed, but he would limit his curse. He said she would have to stay in the mortal world till a garland of celestial flowers fell on her.

Thus, she was born as the princess of the King of Vidarbha as Indumati. It was after a good long time that the garland fell on her and marked the end of her curse. Thus, her existence on this worldly plane had come to an end.

End of King Aja

After narrating this story of Indumati to the King, Sage said, *"O King, enough of brooding with her loss, unhappiness strikes to all those who are born, but being the king, you are bound to show your courage and wisdom to your subjects. You won't be able to regain her by weeping. Death is bound for those who take birth. O the glorious one, you do not deserve to go into grief like an ordinary man."*

The King continued to rule the kingdom till his son Dasharatha was ready to take over, but his heart was still filled with grief over his wife's departure. The death of his beloved wife was eating him from inside. Once his son was ready to be crowned, he entrusted him with the duties of protecting his subjects to his son. He then left the palace, went to the banks of the Sarayu River, and decided to undergo severe penance. He thus attained a place among the immortals.

Chapter 16

King Dasharatha:
The King of Integrity

King Dasharatha and the Kingdom of Ayodhya

After the departure of King Aja, King Dasharatha took over the reign of the kingdom of Ayodhya, also known as Kosala. From the city of Ayodhya, King Dasharatha ruled the entire world. King Dasharatha was well-versed in Vedas and commanded all resources, including scholars, riches, and great forces. Like his ancestors, he was also dearly loved by his people. Among the Ikshvakus, he was a great chariot warrior, capable of fighting many warriors single-handedly. He was a skilful warrior and a farsighted King. His troops were abundant with warriors who were experts in the science of weapons.

The King performed many sacrifices and practised dharma. He was a saintly King who performed many Vedic rituals. He had perfect control of his senses. King Dasharatha was known to keep his promises and never wavered from them. In richness, he was comparable to Indra and Kubera. During his reign, even the people of his kingdom were virtuous and well-read in Vedas and Shastras. They were self-content and happy and free from covetousness. It is said that, in the whole city, one could not find a house without adequate food or wealth or a person who did not follow dharma. All men and women were of righteous conduct and good behaviour. There were no thieves, greedy people, or illiterate people. Every citizen performed their duties as per their Varnas.

The city was ably governed by the most intelligent and foremost among men, King Dasharatha. The mighty Dasharatha defeated all enemies, and he equalled Indra in splendour. The ministers of his council, too, were very virtuous, skilled in their responsibilities, devoted and loyal to the Kingdom. Prominent among them were Dhristi, Jayanta, Vijaya, Siddhartha, Arthsadaka, Ashoka, Mantrapala and Sumantra. The priests for the family were Sage Vashishta and Vamadeva, who were well-versed in all branches of knowledge. King Dasharatha thus became well-known in three worlds as just king, upholder of dharma and protector of his people.

The Story of Shravan Kumar

On a highly delightful morning, King Dasharatha, armed with a bow and arrow, decided to go hunting. He thus rode his chariot towards the river Sarayu. Hiding in the woods, he was waiting for animals to reach the bank of the river. In the darkness, out of his sight, he heard water being disturbed by something. Thinking it to be a wild animal who had come drinking water, he seized his arrow and aimed towards the direction of the sound. But instead of the animal, he heard the cry of a human in pain, and he rushed towards the cry.

The injured person was crying aloud, *"I had come to this lonely place to take some water. Who has hit me? What harm have I done to anyone? I was living the life of an ascetic (rishi). Whoever it is has done a grave sin. I do not regret losing my life, but it's about who will take care of my mother and father in my absence. This arrow has not only killed me but my aged parents as well."* Hearing this cry, the king was stuck in grief. Distressed, the King reached the sight where the boy was lying.

🕉

Seeing the king, the boy further said, "*O King, you shot me when I was trying to fill the pitcher with water for my parents. I am a forest dweller by the name of Shravan Kumar. With this, you have also killed my aged and blind parents. What harm have I done to you? My parents are too weak, and they cannot even walk. My thirsty parents must be waiting for me to bring them water. O King Dasharatha, go and inform my father at once. Go and beg for his forgiveness before he curses you in anger. Before you go, gently remove the arrow from my chest.*"

The king thought if the arrow was not removed, it would be painful; if removed, the boy would die instantly. Seeing the anguish and distress of the King, the boy told him not to feel guilty as he was calm now. He urged the king to remove the arrow. The King then removed the arrow. The boy immediately succumbed to death, and the King was shaken completely.

Having committed the sin unintentionally, he took a pitcher and filled it with clean water from the Sarayu River and went to the hermitage with a heavy heart. In the hermitage, he saw the weak, old, and blind parents of Sharavan Kumar sitting, waiting for their son to arrive and quench their thirst. Hearing the footsteps, the father of the boy said, "*O son, why are you late? Bring me the water quickly.*" The king remained in complete silence, stuck in his grief, and his heart got heavier and heavier every moment. Since the parents didn't feel the son coming, they said, "*O son, don't take to your heart if me or your mother has said something that is disagreeable. You are our only support; you are our eyes. Why are you not saying anything, my dear son?*"

After controlling his mind and a lot of thought in a stammering voice, the king related the entire story to the old parents. He told them that their son was killed by his ignorance and asked them about his next course of action. Grief-stricken ascetic, with tears rolling down their eyes, said, *"If you hadn't broken this news yourself to us, we would have been cursed to have your head shattered to a hundred thousand pieces. This is what happens if a knower of Vedas uses a weapon on a person observing austerities. Since you have done it unknowingly, you are alive. We wish that you would take us to the place where my son's blood-spattered body is lying."*

Thereafter, the King took the mother and father of Shravan Kumar to the place where their son's body was lying. He then assisted them in touching the body of their son. Feeling their son's body, both collapsed and started crying aloud about who would take care of him and his wife, as both were incapable of doing any work. The father and mother, after completing the funeral rites, told the King, *"Kill me, O King, with the same arrow that you used to kill our son. Though you have killed my son unintentionally, I curse that just as I am suffering the grief of my son's death, you will also die of sorrow on account of the separation from your son."* Having cursed King Dasharatha, the old couple laid down their life on the same funeral pyre and went to heaven.

King Dasharatha's Putrakameshti Yajna

King Dasharatha was married to Kaushalya, the princess of Koshala. But they didn't have a son. He married Kaikeyi, the brave princess of Kekaya. He then married Sumitra, but still no son was born to them. He called upon all the great sages and told them that he had no son, and this was the cause of his intense suffering. So, he suggested to them to perform austerities in a Vedic manner.

Then, the King's charioteer narrates to him the story of sage Rishyasringa, who was the son of Vibhandaka, son of Sage Kashyapa. Growing up in the forest, Rishyasringa didn't know anyone else in the world other than his father. He grew up to be a great sage who was well-known in all three worlds. During that period, a great and powerful king lived in the kingdom of Anga, King Romapada. But once, a terrible drought hit his country. He was grief-struck, the king summoned all learned and wise sages. They suggested bringing Rishyasringa, honouring him, and giving him the King's daughter, Shanta, in marriage.

After convincing his councillors to bring the great Sage to the kingdom, they devised a plan to bring the great sage. As soon as the sage set foot in the kingdom of Anga, it started raining. The King offered his daughter in marriage to the Sage. The charioteer of King Dasharatha told the King that if this Rishi was brought there for the yajna, The King would be blessed with a great son.

King Dasharatha then met his friend Romapada and expressed his desire to take Sage Rishyasringa and his wife Shanta to Ayodhya to perform the sacrificial rites to obtain a son. Sage Rishyasringa agreed to the same. They arrived at the city of Ayodhya, where Shanta was well received by the queens of Ayodhya. The Sage had told the King that he would get the desired results if the procedure were performed without any hindrance, and he must be sure about it. Sage Rishyasringa then told the queen that all materials for the rites were to be procured, and the sacrificial horse would be released. The rites were started, and the ministers and soldiers were explained their responsibilities.

After one year of the sacrificial rites and no hindrance, on an auspicious day, along with the best of Brahmins led by Sage Vashishta, headed by Sage Rishyasringa, King Dasharatha entered the sacrificial pavilion. The Brahmans who conducted the rites were given a lot of wealth. Sage Rishyasringa said to

the king, *"O King, so be it, four great sons will be born to you. Now that any sins have been purged out, I will now begin the Putrakameshti yajna, a sacrifice for begetting children."* The Sage then commences the Putrakameshti Yajna.

During the sacrifice, a mighty being emerged from the sacrificial fire with a pot filled with payasam (a preparation of rice in milk and sugar), which was handed over to King Dasharatha. He told the King to give it his worthy consorts as this would help him bear sons. The king took the pot and went to his queens. The King gave Kaushalya a half portion of the payasam. He then gave a part of it to Sumitra and another part to Kaikeyi. He then gave the remaining part to Sumitra.

Having been honoured by the King, all assembled kings returned to their kingdom pleased. Having duly honoured, sage Rishyasringa and his wife, along with King Romapada, set out for his country. King Dasharatha, with his desire to fulfil his thoughts, centred around begetting sons, lived happily. Soon, news of the queen getting pregnant spread across the city. The King and the citizens were equally happy hearing this, and celebrations began.

Chapter 17

Shree Rama:
The Cause of Delight

The Incarnation of Supreme MahaVishnu

As the Putrakameshti Yajna was going on in the hall of King Dasharatha, at the same time, all Devatas, along with Gandharvas, assembled in front of Lord Brahma and said, "O Lord, a Rakshasa named Ravana, who had received a *boon from your grace is now harassing and oppressing us. He is inflicting pain in three worlds. Because of the boon from you, he has become unassailable. O Lord, please find some means to kill him.*" Ravana was granted the boon, and he could not be killed by Devatas, Asuras, Rakshasa, Danavas, Gandharvas, or Yakshas. But he didn't include humans due to his ignorance. Brahma then assures the assembled ones that Ravana can be killed by humans and no one else. Hearing this, everyone was overwhelmed.

At the same time, The Supreme MahaVishnu arrived there on his Garuda. MahaVishnu then met Lord Brahma and the Devatas. Devatas offered Him prayer and described to him how Ravana was tormenting them and prayed to MahaVishnu to take human form and be born as a son to the three wives of King Dasharatha, who was a righteous person as one can be and eliminate Ravana. The omnipotent and omnipresent Supreme Lord agreed to incarnate himself in a fourfold way as the son of King Dasharatha.

When the Lord decided to incarnate as the son of King Dasharatha, Lord Brahma then addressed the Devatas, *"Create strong and powerful helpers capable of taking any forms and support Lord Vishnu. Create sons who are powerful, capable of changing forms, who have a speed of light, intellect, knowledgeable, and knower of various kinds of weapons. Incarnate them in the wombs of Apsaras, Gandharvas, vannariyas, etc. I have already created mighty Jambhavan, foremost among bears."*

Instructed by Lord Brahma, the Devatas gave birth to sons in the form of vanaras. Maharishis and Siddhas procreated heroic sons who became forest dwellers. Indra gave birth to Vali, with the mighty body, while Surya Dev (Sun God) begot Sugriva. Similarly, Brihaspati begot highly intelligent Tara, Kubera to glorious Gandhmadana, Vishvakarma to great Nala, while Agni begot powerful Neel. Ashvinikumars gave birth to Mainda and Dwivid. Varuna begot Sushena and Parjanya to strong Sharabh. Vayu gave birth to Hanuman, who was mighty, dignified, graceful, and had a body as strong as a diamond and speed equal to Garuda. Among all, he was the most intelligent and strong. Thus, thousands of warriors were born on earth and assembled to kill Ravana.

In the twelfth month of Chaitra, on the ninth day of Shuklapaksh, Queen Kaushalya gave birth to a son, Shree Rama, Lord MahaVishnu's incarnation. As the incarnation of one-fourth of Vishnu, imbibed with all virtues and righteousness, Bharata was born to Queen Kaikeyi. After this, Queen Sumitra gave birth to two sons – Lakshmana and Shatrughna – who were skilled in the use of all weapons. Thus, four worthy sons were born to King Dasharatha, and all three worlds rejoiced. Ayodhya went into festive mode as the King distributed gifts among his citizens. After eleven days, Sage Vashishta held the naming ceremony as per Vedic samskaras. As time passed, the sons of King Dasharatha grew, and all the rites were duly performed. King Dasharatha bestowed the Brahmins and others of the city generously with wealth.

Shree Rama and Vishvamitra

All four sons of King Dasharatha became well-versed in the Vedas. They were courageous, strong and endowed with knowledge and wisdom. They were profound in the art and science of weapons. They were devoted to the welfare of the people. They were very modest, farsighted and very dear to the people. Among the four, Rama was highly radiant and mighty, free from any moral stains, virtuous and became very dear to his father. Since its early days, Lakshmana has remained very close to Rama. He loved Rama as though Rama was his life, and similarly, Rama was also very fond of Lakshmana. In the same manner, Shatrughna became dear to Bharata and vice versa.

One day, Sage Vishvamitra, the son of Gadhi, visited King Dasharatha. He was well received and given honour by the king. The King then asked Sage, *"O Brahman, how fortunate I am to have you here! What is your desire, and in what way can I fulfil your desire?"* The Sage then replied, *"O Great King, I have come for a purpose. Be truthful to your promise and take a decision. I was carrying out a sacrifice, but the two rakshasas, Marich and Subahu, who can assume any form, would create obstruction. I am nearing the completion of the sacrifice, but these demons have rained blood and flesh over the sacrificial altar. Since I am involved in this sacrifice, I cannot curse anyone, nor can I use weapons on anyone. Kindly entrust your elder son Rama to me, and his valour can destroy those demons. You can be sure that I will protect him. O King, those demons cannot withstand the mighty Rama. So, keep aside the love for your son and fulfil your promise."*

ॐ

Having heard the Sage, the King experienced intense grief and was terribly upset. The King said that Rama was still a child. The King himself, along with his army, would come along with the Sage and protect the sacrificial ritual. On hearing the King's reluctance to comply with the wish, Sage Vishvamitra was angry and started to leave, saying that the King was unable to keep his promise. Sage Vashishta said to the King that Rama was well-trained and courageous and assured him that Rama would be protected by Vishvamitra himself. He then further added that the king born in the Ikshvaku race should always keep his promise. Sage Vashishta then explained to the King the greatness of Vishvamitra and his capability of using any kind of weapon, saying that it would be for the benefit of Prince Rama that he chose Rama for this job. Satisfied by the explanation, the King permitted Shree Rama to go with Vishvamitra.

Shree Rama, accompanied by his brother Lakshmana, followed the Sage Vishvamitra. On reaching the banks of the Sarayu River, the Sage told Prince Rama to take some water in his hand, and then taught him the mantra – Bala and Atibala. He then said, *"If you receive this mantra, you will never be fatigued or feel hungry, nor will there be any change in your appearance. No one can harm you, even in your sleep. Your valour, kindness or wisdom in this world cannot be matched by anyone in this world."*

As they travelled further, they reached the forest where Tataka, wife of Daitya Sunda and mother of Marich, lived. Vishvamitra then ordered Shree Rama to kill the yakshini Tataka, who is wicked and extremely cruel and powerful. Yakshini Tataka had become a demoness by the curse of Agatsya Rishi. Rama then killed Tataka, who was raining boulders on Rama and Lakshmana. Rejoicing the death of Tataka, the Devatas gave Sage Vishvamitra permission to give Shree Rama celestial weapons. Sage then gave to Shree Rama the Dandachakra, Dharmachakra,

Kalachakra, Vishnuchakra, IndrAstra, VajrAstra, Shiva's trident, BrahmashirAstra, AishikAstra and BrahmaAstra along with Modaki, Shikhari and many more unique weapons. Sage then taught Shree Rama the methods to invoke dispatch and withdraw the weapons.

After this, they passed the hermitage of Siddhashram, where Lord Vishnu practised austerities during His incarnation as Vamana. It was here that Lord Vishnu took birth as the son of Sage Kashyapa and Devi Aditya and assumed the form of Vamana. In this incarnation, He subdued King Bali and helped Indra get back his kingdom, thereby restraining Bali's energy. It was here that Sage Vishvamitra had been doing his sacrificial rituals. Rama and Lakshmana were vigilant during the sacrifice procedure and waited for the rakshasas to come. As sacrifice was being performed, suddenly flesh and blood started raining. Rama, then using the ManavAstra, threw Marich hundreds of miles away and, using AgniAstra, killed Subahu.

After killing the Rakshasas, later that night Shree Rama and Lakshmana approached Sage and enquired about the next move. The Sage then told them that it was now their turn to visit the King of Mithila, Janaka, who was performing a religious sacrifice. The sacrifice was being performed on magnanimous bow, which none could string.

Along their journey, they reached the hermitage of the illustrious Sage Gautama. Sage Vishvamitra narrated the story of Sage Gautam and Mata Ahalya. One day, in the absence of Sage Gautama, Indra disguised himself, taking the form of Sage Gautama, approached Mata Ahalya and expressed his desire to have a union with her. Ahalya, who was proud of her beauty, though recognised Indra, accepted the offer. After the union, as Indra was about to leave, Sage Gautama entered the hut and saw both inside the hut. Through his powers, he understood what had happened and, therefore, cursed both Indra and Ahalya. Sage had cursed Ahalya to stay in that hut for thousands of years, invisible to everyone, sustaining only on air, without food. Sage told her that she would be relieved of her curse only when Shree Rama visited the place and after she honoured Him. She will then regain her original body and will be able to come to him (Sage Gautama). Indra had done this with the intention of obstructing Sage Gautama's sacrifice as he was frightened of his powers. Shree Rama, along with Sage Vishvamitra, entered the hermitage. Ahalya's curse came to an end, and she became visible. Shree Rama and Lakshmana then touched her feet. She then extended her hospitality according to the tradition. Ahalya was finally united with their husband, Sage Gautama, after years of separation and penance.

Marriage of Devi Sita and Shree Rama

Sage Vishvamitra, Shree Rama, and Lakshmana moved ahead and finally reached King Janaka's palace. The great Sage was duly received and honoured by the King himself. King Janaka then enquired with Sage about the two young men. Sage then introduced them as the illustrious sons of King Dasharatha. He further added that they had accompanied him to kill the rakshasas who were creating trouble while performing his rituals, and in the course of their journey to Mithila, they met Ahalya and Sage Gautama. The virtuous King Janaka then paid respect and welcomed Sage Vishvamitra and the two young princes.

King Janaka asked the Sage the reason for their arrival. The sage then replied that the princes have a desire to see the magnanimous bow. They were curious about the great bow under your custody and hence had accompanied me. The King then said, "*O Adorable ones, once there was a King in our lineage named Devarata, who was the eldest son of Nimi. This Bow was entrusted to him by the Supreme Lord Shiva. It is said that during the devastation of Daksha's sacrifice, Lord Shiva, in anger, lifted this bow and told other Devatas that even he desires to partake in the share of the sacrifice. Since it wasn't shared, he sportingly threatened to sever their heads. All Devatas then prayed to the Supreme Shiva. Shiva pleased with them, gave them his divine bow, and who then bestowed it my ancestor.*"

The King continued further, "*One day, I was ploughing my farm to prepare for austerities. At that moment, from the ploughed ground, a baby girl appeared, and she was named Sita since she rose from the earth through ploughing and not from the womb. I raised her as my own daughter. I have decided to give her in marriage to a person who will be able to lift the bow and string it. Many eminent princes came with a desire to marry my daughter, but none of them could even lift the bow. Thereafter, all kings, inflamed with anger, had even tried to attack Mithila but failed in their mission. I shall show this bow to the prince Rama and Lakshmana. O Sage, if Rama can lift the bow and string it, I shall give my daughter to Rama in marriage.*"

The King then ordered the bow to be brought and shown to Shree Rama. With great difficulty, five thousand stalwarts of the king brought in an iron cart, the bow, which hosts of mighty kings, devatas, asuras, etc., failed to lift. The divine bow was kept in front of Shree Rama. Shree Rama then asked permission from Sage to touch it, lift it and string it. On obtaining Sage Vishvamitra's permission, Shree Rama picked up the bow with ease and strung it in the presence of thousands of men. After stringing it, as he drew the string back, the bow broke into two from the middle, generating a loud sound like the trembling of the earth. On seeing this, King Janaka was pleased. The King asked Sita for her acknowledgement regarding the marriage. After Sita Devi also gave her nod for the alliance, The King sent his councillors to Ayodhya to communicate the events to King Dasharatha and invite him to Mithila.

Pleased to hear the message, King Dasharatha, along with Sage Vasishta, other relatives, and the army, arrived in Videha. King Janaka then appropriately welcomed everyone. Following this, King Janaka gave the hand of his daughter Sita to Rama and younger daughter Urmila to Lakshmana. King Janaka's younger brother, Khushadwaja, had two daughters who were unrivalled in beauty. He wished to marry his two daughters to the brilliant princes of Ayodhya, Bharata and Shatrughna. King Dasharatha agreed to the alliance of Shrutakirti with Bharata and Mandavi with Shatrughna. The marriage ceremony of all four princes and princesses was thus completed in a grand ceremony. The next day, the great Sage Vishvamitra blessed the princes born in the race of Raghu. He then took leave of the two Kings and set out to the Northern Himalayas. King Dasharatha, along with sons and daughters-in-law, maharishis, and the army, left for Ayodhya.

Shree Rama Encounters Parashurama

As the King, princes, and their army passed through the forest, they heard the frightening sound of birds and beasts moving along the right side of the troop. The King then enquired the same to Sage Vashishta, who told him it was a sign of great danger, but the animals' movement indicated a speedy end to the fears. Suddenly, the area was covered with dust and darkness. The entire troop, except for the Sage Vasishta and other sages, King, his sons, and his daughters-in-law, suddenly fell unconscious. From the cloud of dust, the descendant of Bhrigu and son of Jamadagini, the slayer of Kshatriyas, the great Parashuram appeared, looking like a flaming fire. All the saints then addressed him in a soothing word: *"Rama! Rama!"*.

The great Parashurama, having accepted the homage paid by the Sage, said to Shree Rama, *"O Son of Dasharatha! I have come to know of your prowess and the news of you breaking the great Shiva's great bow, which is a great feat. Thus, I have brought you another great bow. This is the bow of Parashurama, show your power by stringing this bow, fixing the arrow on this bow and stretching it. After this, I will engage in a duel with you."* Hearing this, King Dasharatha pleaded to Parashurama, *"O Brahmana, highly renowned one and now that you have withdrawn your anger towards kshatriyas and have renounced arms, I beg for the life of my sons."*

Ignoring the words of the King, he told Shree Rama, *"These two great bows were made by Vishvakarma, the greatest of all and divine. One that you broke was used by Lord Shiva to kill Tripurasura. The second one belongs to Lord Vishnu, which is equally strong. This bow, capable of conquering hostile cities, was given to Richika of the Bhrigu race and was then passed on to his son and my father, great Jamadagini. Renouncing his weapons, and while he was meditating, Kritaveeryarjun killed him by foul means. Hearing this, enraged, I killed Kshatriyas again and again and conquered the entire world. After this, I made a sacrifice, donated the earth to Sage Kashyapa, and made Mahendra Mountain my abode. Having heard that you have broken Shiva's bow, I have come here. Take this bow of Lord Vishnu inherited by me, fix an arrow and engage in a duel with me if so."*

Hearing this, Shree Rama said, *"I appreciate the marvellous act done by you to repay your father's debt (Pitr debt). Out of respect, I have been patiently listening to you, but you have been underrating me. I am a Kshatriya of the Suryvanshi race, and now you will see my valour and shine."* Enraged, with quick vigour, Shree Rama took the bow and arrow from Parashurama's hand. Shree Rama then fixed the arrow on the bow and told Parashurama, *"You are Brahmin and are related to Sage Vishvamitra; I will not release this arrow towards your body. Since once the bow is fixed on this great bow, it cannot go in vain. So, I give you two options: either I destroy your capability to move quickly at any place at any time, or I destroy the ascetic power which you have gained in three worlds through your austerities."*

Beholding this sight of Shree Rama holding this great bow, Lord Brahma, along with all Devatas, Gandharva, Apsaras, Siddhas, Kinnaras, Yakshas, Rakshasas and Nagas, arrived there. Subdued by Rama's ability, paralysed Parashurama spoke in a gentle voice, *"When I handed over the earth to Kashyapa, he had told me that I should not stay in his country. I had then promised him that I would not stay here during the night as Earth now belongs to him. So, please don't destroy my mobility. I will quickly leave for Mahendra Mountain with the speed of mind. You may destroy the merits which I have conquered through my ascetic power. Please don't delay it. I have come to understand that you are Lord Vishnu himself. I accept my defeat to the ruler of all worlds, and I am not embarrassed by it. Now you me release the bow on me while I shall return to Mahendra Mountain at once."*

Shree Rama then released the bow and destroyed the merits acquired by Parashurama's ascetic power. The darkness then disappeared, and all Devatas were pleased. Having praised Shree Rama, Parashurama returned to his abode.

Shree Rama's Return to Ayodhya

King Dasharatha then embraced and kissed his son and ordered his troops to advance to Ayodhya. The King and his princes were well received in the city while Kaushalya, Sumitra and Kaikeyi were busy receiving the new brides.

After a few days, King Dasharatha one day told Bharata that his maternal uncle Yudhajit, had come to take him to his place. Bharata then along with Shatrughna prepared for his journey. Meanwhile Rama and Lakshmana continued to serve their father and mothers, while discharging their duties toward their kingdom. Sita became Rama's beloved wife with her virtue and their affection towards each other reached new heights each passing day.

Rama never told lies and always honoured elders. He loved his people as much as his people loved him. He was kind-hearted, righteous, self-restraint, pure and honoured the code of conduct of Kshatriyas. He was skilled and encouraged righteousness, while punishing the wicked in an appropriate manner.

King Dasharatha, feeling his ageing body in consultation with his councillors, decided to coronate the worthy Rama. King then summons various kings, his ministers, and councillors and addresses them, *"Having lived in this body for long enough, I would like to rest. I always desired the welfare of the entire world and the happiness of the people. Following the path of my forefathers, I intend to install my son Rama to look after the welfare of the people, who have inherited every virtue and are equal to Indra in prowess. Although this decision is my opinion, I would like to get your consent and have you tell me what is to be done."* Brahmins, kings, other great people, and the citizens of his kingdom were unanimous with the decision of their king and agreed to coronate Rama.

King then tells Sage Vashishta and others to start the preparation for coronation ceremony. Meanwhile Rama was also informed about the decision. After which Rama along with Sumitra, Sita and Lakshmana go to meet Mother Kaushalya to take her blessings. Having heard about the coronation, the citizens, filled with joy, began to decorate the city.

Chapter 18

Shree Rama:
Exiling of Righteous Rama

Queen Kaikeyi's Boon

The city of Ayodhya was decorated with flowers and the path to the palace was sprinkled with water mixed with sandalwood. The banners and flags were placed everywhere; the city was shining like the brightest of sun in galaxy. The temples of the city were cleaned and painted and brahmins were given sweets by Shree Rama. The citizens were overjoyed with the celebrations. All kinds of musical instruments were being played around the city.

This magnificent scene was being watched from the top of the palace by Manthara, Queen Kaikeyi's maid, who had been with her since childhood. Astonished by this sight, the hunchback maid, Manthara, enquired to another royal maid about the reason for the decorations and donations. Bursting with joy, the royal maid told Manthara that everyone was waiting for Shree Rama's arrival. They also informed us that Shree Rama would be announced as the heir to the throne the next day.

Hearing this, the furious Manthara ran down from there to Queen Kaikeyi and said, *"O fool! Get up. Why are you sleeping? You are going to be in great trouble. Your husband treats you like his favourite, but the fact is that he dislikes you."* On being enquired by the Queen, the cunning Manthara, who is very skilled in speech, further said, *"Your good fortune is coming to an end. King is crowning Shree Rama as his heir. I always seek your well-being, and hence, I feel like I am being consumed by fire. Your husband speaks of being moral, but in fact, he is deceitful. Today, he is going to bestow all benefits on Queen Kaushalya. He sent Bharata away, and now he is going to install Rama as his heir. You and your son will be ruined. Get your act together quickly."*

Hearing these words from Manthara, Kaikeyi was overjoyed. She was gifted a beautiful necklace, and thanked her for giving such wonderful news. She said she doesn't see any distinction between Rama and Bharata and hence is full of joy as her beloved Rama is being coronated. Annoyed at this, Manthara threw the necklace and said, *"O naïve Queen, why are you happy instead of being in sorrow? Great misfortune has befallen you. Rama and Bharat are both the rightful heirs to the throne. Shree Rama is afraid of Bharata, and hence, Bharata will be in danger once the insecure Rama gets the throne. Lakshmana is close to Rama's heart, and Lakshmana and Shatrughna are too small, and hence they are not considered a threat to his heir. You will then have to be a slave of Queen Kaushalya, and Bharata will become the slave of Rama. You and your daughter-in-law will be deprived of any happiness."*

To this, Queen Kaikeyi said, *"Rama is righteous, knowledgeable, truthful, grateful and has his senses under his control. He is the eldest son of the King and is deservedly the rightful heir. Rama is worthier than Bharata. Rama serves me more than Kaushalya. Rama regards all his brothers as himself. After Rama's tenure, Bharata will get the throne. For me, both are equal."* Manthara, saddened by these words, again said, *"The son of the King becomes the next heir and not Bharata. Your son will be disheartened and broken. Rama will banish him from his kingdom. You should save him."*

The continuous poisoning of Kaikeyi's mind by Manthara finally had its effect. Kaikeyi, soon burning with anger, told her that Rama would not be coronated and that it would be Bharata instead. She said Rama would be banished from the kingdom. She then started to think about how she could achieve this. To this, the wicked Manthara then told Kaikeyi, *"O Kaikeyi, I will tell how this can be achieved. Long ago, when there was a war between the Devatas and Asuras, your husband took you along with him to assist the Devatas. He took you to the famous city in the south of Dandaka Forest named Vaijayanta, where an Asura named Shamara lived. He was well-versed in various magical spells, such as maya. He had challenged Indra to a battle. The asura used to kill the wounded and fast-asleep soldiers during the night. In that great battle, King Dasharatha was injured by the weapons of Asura and fell unconscious. At that moment, you, who had been his charioteer, saved his life by taking him far away from the battlefield. He was again attacked by asuras, you took him away and saved his life. For this, he granted you two boons out of gratification. You had then told your husband that you would ask for the boon whenever you desired. Now, it is time to ask your husband for those two boons – the coronation of Bharata and the banishment of Rama for fourteen years. Now enter the chamber of King, immersed in grief and tears. King is afraid of your anger; he will forsake his life for your happiness. Make him recollect his boons. He may try to persuade for otherwise but don't pay heed to it. After Rama was exiled for fourteen years, Bharat would have gained the favour of his people and would remain king for the rest of his life. Wearing a soiled dress, lie down on the floor and don't speak to the King. There isn't any doubt that you are the favourite of the King, and seeing you in this state, he would not be able to refuse to fulfil your wishes."*

Thus, Kaikeyi's mind was poisoned by the evil-minded Manthara. Even a wise woman like Kaikeyi succumbed to

Manthara's sinister plans and praised her for her ideas. She told her that once the objectives were accomplished, she would shower gifts on her. The Queen then unfolded her strategy again to Manthara. Manthara was happy and felt as if she had accomplished the objective. With ornaments discarded in soiled cloth, the Queen lay down on the floor.

Exiling of Shree Rama

King Dasharatha, after giving orders for the arrangement of the coronation, entered the palace and entered the chamber of Queen Kaikeyi. He couldn't find his beloved wife anywhere in the chamber and enquired about her whereabouts. The doorkeeper then said that she had gone to her chamber of wrath in a very angry mood. On entering the chamber, the King saw his wife lying down on the floor and enquired about the reason for her present state. The Queen then said, *"O King, I have not been offended or disregarded by anyone. I have something to be fulfilled, which I will reveal only if you promise to do so."* The King then assured her that he would fulfil her desire.

Delighted by the words of the King, the Queen then disclosed her dreadful wish by reminding him of the boons which he had given her in the presence of thirty-three Devatas, including Indra. She told him that Bharata should be coronated and Rama to be sent immediately to Dandaka Forest for fourteen years and live like an ascetic.

Hearing these words, the King was extremely distressed and said, *"O cruel and wicked lady, you are keen on destroying this family. What harm has been done to you by me or Rama? He has always treated you as his mother. When the whole world is singing praise of his virtue, for what crime should I abandon him? I shall give up everything, but I cannot leave my Rama. Rama is a hero who has won the people's hearts through truthfulness, the poor through charity, the preceptors through service, and enemies through battle. He has done more service to you than Bharata. O lady, give up your evil intentions."*

The queen then said, if he repents on giving boons, how shall he be a righteous person? Even after repeated pledging and falling on her feet, the queen remained adamant on her words. The king fell unconscious but, on regaining consciousness, tried to persuade the Queen to abandon her wicked plans. But all his pleas fell on deaf ears.

The preparations for coronation were in full swing throughout the kingdom. Vedic chants were being continuously performed. The next day, early morning, when Sage Vashishta came in a very happy state, he sent Sumantra, the King's charioteer, to awaken the King. Kaikeyi then instructed Sumantra to summon Shree Rama at once. Unaware of her malicious intention, filled with delight, Sumantra rushed into Rama's palace and conveyed the King and Queen's message. On seeing Rama alongside Sita, he informed them that the King and Queen Kaikeyi desired to see them as soon as possible. Adorned in auspicious ornaments, Rama took leave of Sita and accompanied Sumantra to the King's palace.

As Rama entered the chamber, he saw the King in a miserable state with a pale face, seated next to Kaikeyi. Rama, with utmost humility, touched their feet and enquired about the pale state of his father. Rama asked why his father was not reciprocating his greetings and asked if he had committed any offence. He then put forth the same question to Kaikeyi, who unhesitantly said, *"King is neither angry nor has any misfortune befallen on him. You must fulfil the promise he had made to me."* She then told him about the boon the king had given her and about her wish to exile him from the kingdom and coronate Bharata.

Hearing this, Rama did not fall in grief; in fact, he replied, *"Be it so. I shall go to the forest and live like an ascetic to keep my father's promise. Ordered by my father, who is my well-wisher and guru, I will not hesitate to carry out the same. I shall have gladly given the kingdom to my brother Bharata. With the King's order, the messengers should immediately leave to fetch Bharata from uncle's house. After taking leave of my mother and consoling Sita, I will immediately leave for the forest for fourteen years."* Shree Rama bowed at the feet of King and Queen Kaikeyi and set out. Lakshmana, who had accompanied Rama, was filled with tears in his eyes and followed Shree Rama in rage.

Rama, Sita and Lakshmana's Departure

The news of Rama's banishment reached the people. Tormented in grief, the King sank into his seat. Entering the chamber of his mother, Kaushalya, Rama touched her feet and sought permission for his departure. Hearing this, Kaushalya fell to the ground and was then raised up by Shree Rama, who also wiped her tears and consoled her. While Kaushalya was lamenting, Lakshmana asked Rama to assume the authority of the kingdom with force, and he said he would assist him. Queen Kaushalya, also in support of Lakshmana, said that Rama should do what is right and she cannot permit him to go to the forest. Shree Rama then said that following father's order is the right thing to do. He tells Lakshaman that when an elderly person, whether in anger or pleasure or passion, gives any command, then it should be followed as our dharma. He tells Lakshmana it is his destiny to go to the forest, and if not, how could Mother Kaikeyi, who had never differentiated between him and Bharata, prevent his coronation and send him into the forest?

Rama again requested his mother, Kaushalya, for her permission to leave for the forest. Kaushalya then insisted on taking her too to the forest as well. Rama then declines her, saying that service to her husband is the supreme virtue. Kaushalya, filled with tears in her eyes, grants Rama permission and gives her blessings. Shree Rama then enters his palace with a sorrowful face, where Sita is engaged in thoughts of coronation. On being enquired by Sita, Rama then narrates the entire episode of banishment to her. He also tells Sita that she should practice dharma and never expect special treatment from Bharata, take care of the King and Queen, and perform one's duties righteously.

Sita then tells Rama that the wife alone shares the destiny of her husband, and hence, she is also ordered to go to the forest with him. Sita then pleads to take her along with him, but Rama, unwilling to take her, tries to persuade her by describing the hardship in the forest. Having heard this, Sita, in a faint voice, says, *"I very well understand the difficulties in the forest, but I will be able to survive it accompanied by your affection. If separated from you, I shall give up my life. You should not depart to the forest without taking me. You shall not anticipate any problem because of me."* Finally, after repeated pleading, Rama agrees to take her with him. Delighted, Sita prepared to leave by giving away all her jewels and ornaments.

Lakshmana, who by then had arrived there, unable to bear the grief, held his brother's feet and told him that wherever they went, he would accompany them by walking before them, holding the bow. Rama tried to discourage Lakshmana by asking if he accompanied them, who would take care of Mother Kaushalya Sumitra and their father? Lakshmana then says Bharata will definitely take care of them, and Mother Kaushalya is competent enough to support herself. She requests Rama to allow him to follow them. Rama then acknowledges and allows him to accompany them.

Rama, Sita and Lakshmana then pay homages to all learned brahmins, distributes their wealth to all the brahmins, attendants, poor people. All three of them, dressed as ascetics, visits King Dasharatha who was lying unconscious in the chamber was picked by them. Rama then asks permission to leave for the forest along with Sita and Lakshmana. Sage Vasishta tried to stop Sita from going to the forest, but she was not willing to let go of her resolve.

Thereafter, Rama, Sita and Lakshmana with folded hands touched the feet of king and paying respect to Mother Kaushalya and Sumitra boarded the chariot secured with weapons set out for the forest. The entire city was distressed, and everyone ran behind the chariot. Meanwhile the King denounces Kaikeyi and reaches for Kaushalya. As Kaushalya was lamenting, she was consoled by Sumitra.

On reaching the banks of river Tamasa, Rama, Lakshmana and Sita decide to spend their first night of exile there. Rama and Sita spent their night on the bed of leaves prepared by Sumantra. As Rama and Sita fell asleep, Lakshmana, who was awake, spent the night describing Rama's virtue to Sumantra. At the onset of dawn, Rama saw the citizens of Ayodhya fast asleep, so he told Sumantra and Lakshmana, *"Look at these people fast asleep under the trees, following us out of affection towards us and unmindful of their home. On seeing the people's resolve, they would not abandon their decision. While they are asleep, we shall quickly mount on the chariot and move away from here."* Rama, Sita and Lakshmana, along with charioteer Sumantra, silently and speedily crossed the river and sped away. When the citizens woke up, they could not see their beloved Rama; thus, dejected, they returned to the city. On reaching the banks of River Ganga, Rama tells Sumantra that he should return to Ayodhya as they no longer need chariots, and he is preparing to live the life of an ascetic.

Rama Meets Sage Bharadwaja

Shree Rama tried to convince Lakshmana to go back to Ayodhya to take care of his parents and brothers, but Lakshmana said he would never leave his brother Rama and Devi Sita in the forest alone for anyone. Shree Rama then gave him permission to stay with them for the entire period of exile. As the night fell, Shree Rama and Sita fell asleep on a beautiful bed made by Lakshmana under the banyan tree. As the sun rose, the trio made their way deeper into the forest to reach the place where River Bhagirathi meets River Yamuna. By evening, they reached the hermitage of Sage Bharadwaja at the convergence of the Yamuna and Ganga rivers.

Rama entered the hermitage on being invited by Sage's disciples. On entering, he saw Sage Bharadwaja surrounded by his disciples. Rama, Lakshmana and Sita paid respect to the sages and introduced themselves. The Sage then provided them with water, food, and a place to rest. Accepting the hospitality of the Sage, Rama said, *"My city is very near here, and my people will frequently visit me if I stay here. Hence, I do not wish to stay here. Kindly suggest a place that is solitary, and Princess Janaki (Sita) would be comfortable."*

Sage Bharadwaj then suggested a place on place on the mountain called Chitrakoot which was regularly frequented by Maharishis. After spending the night at the hermitage, Shree Rama along with his wife and brother Lakshmana took leave to proceed towards Chitrakoot.

After crossing the Kalinda River and traversing through the forest and they spent the night along the banks of Yamuna River. As they moved further, they reached Chitrakoot and saw a beautiful spot with trees and honeycombs and peacocks. They decide to settle down as their place for completing the exile. They then reached the hermitage of Sage Valmiki and paid due respect and introduced themselves. The righteous Sage Valmiki then honoured them duly.

Shree Rama, shown the right spot by Sage Valmiki, instructed Lakshmana to make a hut so they could spend their period of exile. Lakshmana made a beautiful hut with all the woods. Rama then orders them to get the fruit of gajakand to perform the rituals and pay homage to the Lord prior to beginning their stay. Thus, having reached Chitrakoot, Rama shed his sorrow of banishment and was filled with happiness.

King Dasharatha's Demise

Charioteer Sumanta, on being instructed by Rama, left the banks of the river and reached Ayodhya in three days. He found the entire city cheerless and silent. Depressed and with tears gushing down his eyes, Sumantra drove straight to the palace of King Dasharatha, where all men and women were enquiring about Rama. In the courtyard of the palace, he saw King Dasharatha withered in the sorrow of separation from his beloved son. Sumantra, after paying due respect, conveyed Rama's message. When the king heard about Rama, he was tormented, and he fell down on the ground. Kaushalya and Sumitra lifted him from the ground and burst into tears. All those people who saw weeping Queen Kaushalya and her husband, who had fallen on the ground unconscious, started to cry out loud. After the King regained consciousness, he enquired about Rama's message and wondered how the two young princes and princess of Vaidehi could survive in the forest filled with wild animals and snakes.

With a choked voice and tears, Sumantra said, *"O King, Shree Ramachandra, following the righteousness, with both hands folded and head bowed, said, "O charioteer, convey to my illustrious father who is known for his self-knowledge and one who is worthy, my salutation and touch his feet. Also, give my salutation to all my mothers and talk about my well-being. Tell my mother to conduct myself with my other mothers, including Kaikeyi, without any pride and ego and treat them equally. Treat my young Bharata in the same manner as a king is to be treated, irrespective of age. Tell Bharata also about my well-being, and he should treat all mothers equally. Follow the orders of the aged King and live happily."* Lakshmana then asked why his brother was banished, submitting to the trash command of Mother Kaikeyi. He said, "Rama is alone, my brother, my protector, my friend and my father. How can anyone be pleased with you for deserting the beloved Rama?" Sita didn't say anything, and when I was leaving, she looked at Rama and burst into tears." Sumantra then described events till he turned back and how the city was overcome by a shadow of sorrow.

King Dasharatha again fell unconscious on hearing this. Sumantra then consoled the weeping Queen Kaushalya. Queen Kaushalya also condemns her husband's actions of banishing their son. Hearing the harsh words of Kaushalya, the king went into a deep state of sorrow. The tears gushed down her eyes, and with folded hands, she felt guilty for saying the harsh words to her grief-struck husband. The King then remembered the curse of young Sharavan Kumar's father. The King related the story to Kaushalya and said, *"There is no greater sorrow than not being able to see my righteous Rama again. My heart is sinking, and my senses are giving way. I am going to die."* King Dasharatha, crying in distress in the presence of Kaushalya and Sumitra, gave up his life.

A King of noble vision, grieved by the exiling of his son, tormented by his grief, gave up his life past midnight. Meanwhile, overpowered by grief, the queens were fast asleep. They were awakened by the maids who had come to wake up the King as usual but instead found him breathless. All the queens wept aloud, and Kaushalya even blamed Kaikeyi for the King's death.

Arrival of Bharata

After news of the demise of King Dasharatha, the ministers, councillors, and sages informed Sage Vashishta that a kingdom without a king would put the kingdom into a miserable state. Hence, with Rama and Lakshmana in the forest, the generous Bharata is to be made king. Bharata was living with his maternal uncle at that time, unaware of the turmoil that had happened back home. Sage Vashishta sent his messengers to meet Bharata and Shatrughna and convey the message that the family priest and councillors wished that they should be back urgently for a certain task and told them not to communicate any matters related to Rama and King.

A night before the arrival of messengers from Ayodhya, Bharata had experienced an unpleasant dream, and a great fear had gripped his mind. As he was describing his dreams to his companions, messengers arrived and requested him to immediately return to Ayodhya. Bharata and Shatrughna taking leave from his maternal grandfather, departed and left for Ayodhya.

After seven nights of journey, Bharata reached Ayodhya, where he saw that the city was weeping and cheerless. On entering the palace, he directly went to his father's chamber, and not finding him there, he went to his mother and touched his feet. His mother, Kaikeyi, then enquired about the well-being of his grandfather and uncle, and Bharata narrated everything to her. Bharata then enquired about Ayodhya's sorry state and the missing father. Kaikeyi then revealed that the King was no longer and that Rama, Sita, and Lakshmana had been exiled to Dandaka Forest. Bharata then asked Kaikeyi the reason for Rama's banishment, to which she, assuming that Bharata would be happy to hear, said, "*My son, on hearing about Rama's coronation, I asked your father to hand over the kingdom to you and banish Rama. Faithful to his words, he banished Rama. The great king, unable to hold his grief for his beloved son, gave up his life. For your sake, I have done this. So, get up, my son, give up your sorrow, take control of the kingdom.*"

Hearing this, Bharata said, "*Devoid of my father and my brother, who was like a father, what use is this kingdom for me? You have caused the death of my father and made Rama into an ascetic. You have brought great sorrow to the family and caused the destruction of this race. O sinful woman, I will not be part of your cherished desire, nor am I competent to do this.*" Saying this and much more, Bharata lost consciousness in grief of what had happened. Regaining his consciousness, he then met Kaushalya and Sumitra to appease them and curse himself. Kaushalya was convinced of Bharata's conviction. In the absence of Rama, Sage Vashishta urges Bharata to carry out his father's funeral rites. After thirteen days, seeing the ashes of his father, Bharata and Shatrughna again plunge into sorrow, whereby Sage Vashishta and Sumantra console him.

Shatrughna, who came to know about the deeds of Manthara, in rage, dragged her to Bharata and was about to kill her when Bharata told them that a lady is never to be killed and if Rama comes to know about this, he will never talk to us. Hearing this, Shatrughna restrained his anger and released Manthara.

The next day, all the elders and revered sages who had assembled in the palace urged Bharata to assume the leadership of the kingdom. Bharata then said that he would bring back Rama and in turn he would serve fourteen years in the forest.

Bharata – Rama Meeting

Sage Vashishta requested Bharata to accept the throne, which was passed onto him by King Dasharatha and his brother Rama. Bharata, in a melodious tone, replied, *"O Guru, how could I seize the kingdom which belongs to Rama, who practices brahmachayra, who is well-versed in all kinds of knowledge, who is striving to protect righteousness? How could I seize this kingdom? The eldest, renowned righteous Rama deserves to inherit the kingdom. I will never accept the evil deed committed by my mother. I shall follow Rama; he alone deserves to rule the kingdom. If I am not able to bring back Rama, I will also dwell in the forest with him like the great Lakshmana."* Hearing this, all the men assembled there shed tears of joy, thinking of Rama. Bharata then ordered Sumantra to send the army to find Rama, and he was delighted to receive this order. Bharata also got his chariot ready to go to the forest to meet his brother.

Bharata, along with Shatrughna, Kaushalya, Kaikeyi, Sumitra, and the army, marched towards the forest. Enroute, they met Guha, the lord of Nishadas, and Sage Bharadwaja and enquired about the path to meet Rama. Sage Bharadwaja also told Bharata not to curse his mother, Kaikeyi, as this banishment would lead to a greater cause of happiness in future, and informed him that Rama was staying in Chitrakoot. After paying due homage and thanking them for their hospitality, they left towards Chitrakoot.

As Rama was detailing the beauty of Chitrakoot and River Mandakini to Sita, they heard the noise of the army of Bharata approaching and alerted Lakshmana. Lakshmana mistook the intentions of the approaching army under Bharata and prepared his weapons for battle. He presumed they were coming to kill Rama. Rama then told Lakshmana not to be suspicious of Bharata, as Bharata, not even in his mind, would think of harming them and probably must have come to hand over the kingdom to us as soon as he learned of what happened in Ayodhya.

Seeing Rama, Bharata, overwhelmed in grief, ran towards him, lamenting in misery and crying in distress. Shatrughna also followed suit. Rama then embraced both and enquired about King Dasharatha and Mother Kaushalya, Sumitra and Kaikeyi. He explained his duties toward his citizens and gurus to Bharata. Bharata then pleads to Rama to return to Ayodhya and informs Rama about the demise of their father. Hearing about his father, Rama fell unconscious while Sita started crying. Regaining conscious, he told Lakshmana to gather materials and "ingudi" fruit pulp to offer a libation to their father. Sumantra then helped Rama perform the rites. Seeing his sons performing the rituals, all three mothers were in distress and weeping. They then embraced Sita and Lakshmana and started crying.

Rama touched Sage Vashishta's feet and sat down next to Bharata. On being enquired by Rama about the reason for their arrival, Bharata said that he would like Rama to come back to Ayodhya and get himself coronated, and this is the wish of all three mothers and the subjects who had arrived there. Rama then said, *"O Bharata, I do not see any fault in you, and you should not blame your mother. O Bharata, I have been commanded by our righteous father and mother to go to the forest, and hence, I cannot act otherwise. You shall rule the kingdom of Ayodhya, and I will be in Dandaka Forest."* Bharata then said he wished to return the kingdom to Rama, which was bestowed upon him. Even after repeated pleading, Rama rejected and said that he should go back to Ayodhya, along with Shatrughna, mothers and priests and people who had come there and take command as per their father's wish and become supreme king while Rama shall enter the Dandaka Forest.

The people who listened to them were dejected as Rama was not returning but were delighted to see their favourite Rama's resolve. Rama then said, *"Truth is the greatest virtue. Truth is God and is the foundation of dharma. Charity, rituals, sacrifice and Vedas – all have their foundation as truth. I am always bound to promise and truth. Hence, I shall not disobey my father. The path to heaven is truthfulness, righteousness, valour, compassion towards all beings, respecting guests and brahmins and God."*

Hearing the words of the two brothers, all the esteemed sages were delighted and requested Bharata to listen to his brother and return. Bharata then requested Rama to place his feet on the sandals. Rama placed his foot on them and gave it to the great Bharata. Bharata then said, *"O great Raghunandan, wearing the dress of an ascetic, residing outside the city for fourteen years, looking for your arrival, I will rule the kingdom, placing the responsibility of the ruling on these sandals. On completion of fourteen years, if I don't see you, I will enter the blazing fire."* Rama agreed and, embracing Bharata and Shatrughna, told them to take care of their mothers. Bharata and Shatrughna, along with their mothers, Sage Vashishta, the priest, and the army, returned to Ayodhya.

After leaving their mother at Ayodhya, Bharata left for Nandigram, placing the sandals on his head, along with Shatrughna and councillors. He coronated the sandals of Rama and, leaving as an ascetic, ruled the city in the name of Rama.

Chapter 19

Shree Rama:
The Years in Exile

Devi Sita – Mata Anusuya Conversation

Khara, a brother of Ravana, was causing trouble to the ascetics in Chitrakoot, and hence, many hermits left the place. Rama initially didn't want to leave the place, but after Bharata's visit, the memory of grief haunted Rama. Hence, Rama, accompanied by Sita and Lakshmana, decided to leave the place. Soon, they reached the hermitage of Sage Atri. Sage Atri received Rama like a son and extended hospitality, befitting them. Sage Atri called upon his wife, Anusuya, who was righteous in every way. Mata Anusuya was the one who, through her intense penance, caused the Mandakini River to flow through an area that had been affected by severe drought for ten years. This led to the growth of forests, thus ending the suffering of the sages. She was illustrious, devoid of anger and worthy of admiration. Sage Atri said to Rama that Sita should converse with her, and Rama acknowledged it.

Devi Sita offered her respect with folded hands to Mata Anusuya and enquired about her well-being. Anusuya was delighted to see Sita and said, *"Respectful Sita, leaving all the relatives and following Rama to the forest – it is truly virtuous. Even if your husband is in a city or forest, is sinful or virtuous, if one is devoted to him, such ladies will always attain the highest. There is no greater friend or well-wisher than the husband. The wicked women who dominate their husbands and follow their bodily desires have no understanding of vice and virtue. Women like you who are endowed with virtue, who perform virtuous deeds, attain heaven. Therefore, always uphold the traditions, be virtuous to your husband, and follow your husband."* Mata Anusuya then explained to Sita the duties of a wife. She gave Sita a divine necklace, dress, jewellery, and perfumed lotion, which will never fade. Sita accepted the gifts and told Anusuya the story of her birth and marriage to Rama. Sita adorned the divine gifts and showed them to Ram, who was pleased to see them. The next day, after getting the blessing of the Sage, the trio entered the forest.

Panchavati – Shree Rama's New Home

As the great Rama, accompanied by Sita and Lakshmana, entered deep into Dandaka Forest, they saw many hermitages. On seeing Rama, they welcomed him and requested his protection from the demons. As they moved further, they were attacked by a demon named Viradh, who, in fact, was a Gandharva cursed by Kubera. His hands were cut by Rama and Lakshmana, and his curse was completed after he was killed by them. As they moved further, they met Sage Sharabhanga, who was preparing to leave his body and attain Brahma-loka. After paying due respect to him, Rama requested a proper place for them to stay, and he said that Sage Sutikshna would guide them to their destination.

Enroute, Rama met some sages who requested him to give protection from demons and Rama had assured them of the same. On meeting Sutikshna, Rama expressed the desire to meet Sage Agastya, who lived somewhere in the same forest. Sutikshna then guided them to Sage Agastya. Sage Agatsya was a great sage who was even served by the Devatas. Such was his might that no liar or cruel and wicked man will be able to survive in his vicinity.

On reaching the hermitage of Sage Agatsya, the mighty Rama touched his feet, and all three of them offered respect to the great Sage. Sage Agatsya then gave Rama the divine bow of Lord Vishnu and two quivers full of divine, inexhaustible arrows and swords. Rama then thanked the great and asked him to direct them to a place with water where they could build their hermitage. Sage Agatsya then directed them to a beautiful place named Panchavati, where there is a great banyan tree. Both the princes and Devi Sita paid respect to the sages and took permission to leave for Panchavati.

On the way to Panchavati, they met the great vulture Jatayu, who introduced himself as their father's friend and told Rama that he would protect Sita while they were away building the hut for themselves. Rama, paying respect to Jatayu and leaving Sita under Jatayu's protection, left. Lakshmana then built a strong hut in a beautiful spot surrounded by trees in full blossom and near the river Godavari. Rama and Sita, upon seeing the ashram, were very happy. They told Lakshmana that he had done a wonderful job. The three lived happily there for many years.

Death of Ravana's Brother – Khara and Dhushana

One day, when Rama was engaged in conversation with his beloved wife in his cottage, there appeared a demoness. Shurpanakha, the sister of mighty Ravana, asked why he was staying in the forest. The ever-truthful Rama narrated everything to her. Overtaken by passion, she told Rama to leave Sita and be her husband. Rama, smiling, replied, *"O respected lady, I am married, and this is my lovely wife. Being a cowife would be very painful for a woman like you. Here is my brother, who is valiant and of good conduct. He is not with his wife and asks him if he is interested.”* Hearing these words, she approached Lakshmana to marry her. Lakshmana replied jokingly, *“How can you be a maid, as I am already dependent on my brother? You may become the younger wife of my brother and live here happily.”* Shurpanakha angrily turned to Rama and said he would eat Sita, then could marry her. As she tried to attack Sita, Lakshmana took out his sword and cut off her nose and ear.

Drenched in blood, roaring in dreadful noise, she went inside the forest to her brother Khara and narrated the incident. Hearing this, full of rage, Khara sends his fourteen demons alongside Shurpanakha to attack Rama. But the demons were killed by Rama. Shurpanakha rushes to Khara and incites him to fight Rama. Khara and Dhushana, the brothers of Ravana, along with their fourteen thousand army, plan to attack Rama. Seeing the army marching towards them, Rama instructed Lakshmana and Sita to take shelter in the cave and told Lakshmana to be ready with a bow and arrows. As the demons showered various weapons towards the invincible Rama, the mighty and angry Rama bent his bow, released thousands of arrows and destroyed all demons. As the battle intensified, Dhushana and Khara, along with the chief of armies, were killed. In the end, all the sages thanked Rama for protecting them.

Akampana, Ravana’s uncle, who was with Khara, reached Lanka and reported the events to Ravana. When Ravana said he would go and kill Rama, Akampana said it was not possible to kill Rama alone. He suggested that Ravana should devise a plan and abduct the gorgeous one whose beauty exceeds that of apsaras or goddesses, Sita. On being separated from Sita, Rama will not be able to survive and die. Ravana, the very next day, reached Marich and told him his plan to abduct Sita. Marich, knowing Rama’s ferocity, advised him to go back to Lanka and drop the plan. Hearing Marich, Ravana then left for Lanka.

Kidnaping of Devi Sita

Frightened by the prowess of the great Rama, Shurpanakha ran to her brother, the mighty Ravana, and showed her body, which was disfigured by Lakshmana, inciting him to kill Rama. On being enquired about by Ravana, Shurpanakha narrates the story of Rama's bravery and how he killed their brothers. She also described Sita's beauty and thereby instigated Ravana to kill Rama and Lakshmana and make Sita his wife as soon as possible. Ravana approached the demon Marich and urged his support in abducting Sita and killing Rama and Lakshmana. He explained his evil plan to Marich. Marich initially tried his best to persuade Ravana to forgo his plan by describing Rama's valour and the consequence of doing such a sinful act. Without listening to his advice, Ravana commanded him to assist in accomplishing his task. He told him to take the form of a golden deer and lure Rama and Lakshmana away from Sita. Marich and Ravana reached the Dandaka Forest on his chariot.

Marich transformed into a golden deer and moved to the entrance of Rama's ashram. Plucking flowers, Sita was amazed to see such a beautiful golden deer and told Rama to fetch it so that it could be their playmate. Lakshmana suspected it to be Marich and informed Rama about it. Rama said he would fetch the deer, and if it was the demon, it ought to be killed. Rama told Lakshmana to protect Sita while he went to fetch the deer. Marich, in the form of a deer, took Rama far away from the ashram. Rama followed the deer and struck an arrow at the deer. Marich, giving up his deer's form prior to dying, cries aloud in a voice similar to Rama so that Lakshmana is drawn away from Sita, saying, *"Hey Sita, Hey Lakshmana."* Hearing this, Rama, terrified of what Sita and Lakshmana might think, rushed back.

ॐ

Meanwhile, back at the hermitage, hearing Rama's cry, Sita thought Rama to be in distress and told Lakshmana to protect him. Lakshmana refused to go but was forced to do so by Sita, who said harsh and unpleasant words. Flooded with sorrow at Sita's harsh words, Lakshmana said there is no one in three worlds capable of encountering Rama, and Rama has entrusted him to protect Sita. Sita again humiliated Lakshmana with her harsh words and decided to give up her life. Lakshmana, dejected seeing Sita crying in distress, and with folded hands and great respect, went in search of Rama.

With no Rama and Lakshmana alongside Sita, Ravana came out of hiding and appeared before her in the form of a sage. Seeing the Sage, Sita honoured him with all hospitality and invited him for food. Sighting an opportunity, Ravana, in his true form, introduced himself and asked Sita to be his queen, which she refused. She even warned him of the consequences of harming her. Overcome by anger, Ravana seized Sita's hair using his left hand and lifted her with his right hand. He then placed her on this chariot (Pushpak Vimana) and flew high up in the sky. Distressed, Sita screamed aloud in agony. While Ravana was carrying her away, Jatayu heard Sita's cry and rushed towards the chariot. Jatayu, the righteous vulture, initially pleads to Ravana to release Sita. When Ravana doesn't agree, Jatayu attacks him with all his valour and wounds Ravana. In the end, Ravana, with his sword, cut off the wings and feet of the bird, who immediately fell to the ground.

As Sita was being taken away, she cried out aloud for Rama and Lakshmana and threw a few of her ornaments into the forest in the hope someone would communicate it to Rama. Ravana on reaching Lanka, showed Sita his palace in order to persuade her to marry him. On being rejected, he sent Sita to Ashoka Vatika, guarded by fierce looking demoness.

In Search of Devi Sita

After killing Marich, as the worried Rama rushed towards their hermitage, they saw Lakshmana coming towards him. Together, they rushed back home and found Sita was missing. Lakshmana then narrated why he had to leave Sita alone. Depressed and weeping, Rama went about searching the vast forest for the princess of Mithila in the hope of finding her. Dejected himself, Lakshmana tries to console his brother while searching the forest. As they were searching, they came across Sita's flowers and broken ornaments spread on the ground leading southwards. As they moved further, they saw the wounded Jatayu, who told them that Sita had been kidnapped by Ravana and in an attempt to rescue her, he engaged in a fight with Ravana, who had fatally injured him. Rama hugged the bird, who dropped dead on the ground. After paying oblation to the dead Jatayu, they moved further south.

As they moved further to Kraunch forest, they encountered demoness Ayomukhi, who wanted to obtain Lakshmana, but the angry Lakshmana killed her. They were attacked by the demon Kabandha, who seized them. As the demon was about to eat them, Rama and Lakshmana cut off his arms from his shoulder. Kabandha then revealed that he was the son of Danu, who was cursed due to his pride in getting a boon from Brahma. He was to be released from his curse when he would be killed by Rama. So, he then requests Rama and Lakshmana to kill him, drop him in a pit and cremate him. As his body was burning, Kabandha regained his natural form and told Rama that in order to get back his wife Sita, he should befriend the Vanar King, the mighty Sugriva. He had been banished by his brother Vali and is staying with four monkeys on the banks of river Pampa. Giving them directions to find Sugriva, Kabandha vanished into thin air.

As the duo reached the west bank of Pampa, they came across the hermitage of Sabari, an accomplished ascetic. On seeing them, Sabari touched the feet of Rama and Lakshmana, washed their feet and gave them water as per tradition. After being asked by Rama if her penance had been completed, she said that her penance would be accomplished by serving Rama. She served Rama with the forest-grown fruits and showed her Matang garden, where her guru used to do austerities and invoke gods. Rama was pleased with her service and told her that her wishes would be fulfilled. By virtue of her self-meditation, she left her body and reached the world where her guru had attained. After her departure, Rama set forth towards the sacred Rishyamukha, where Sugriva was supposed to be hiding.

Killing of Vali

As the deeply sad Rama and Lakshmana moved through the beautiful banks of the Pampa River, they were sighted by the righteous Vanar King Sugriva. Their sight frightened Sugriva, as he presumed them to be sent by Vali to kill him. He told the Son of Vayu, the highly esteemed, most powerful Hanuman, to assume the form of an ordinary man and approach the two men and try to find out the reason for their arrival. Assuming the form of a tapasvi beggar, the mighty, ingenious Hanuman approached Rama and Lakshmana, offered them respect and addressed them in pleasant words, *"You both resemble royal sages, how come you are wandering in this forest? You are radiating like gods, though human warriors, deserving to rule the world, why are you silent? I am Vanara Hanuman, and I am sent here on behalf of the great and righteous warrior Sugriva, who has been wandering in this land and has been banished by his brother. He wishes to extend his friendship towards you. For this, I have come here disguised in this form."* Rama understood that

Hanuman was well-versed in Vedas and grammar; otherwise, he wouldn't have been able to speak with utmost refinement. Rama and Lakshmana expressed their desire to be friends with Sugriva and explained the reason for their arrival. Hanuman then takes them to Sugriva.

On meeting Sugriva and hearing everything from Hanuman, Rama and Sugriva formalised their friendship and assured each other they would help each other. Sugriva then said that when he was sitting on the mountain, he had seen a wicked demon forcefully taking Sita through the sky, and Sita, on seeing him, had dropped her ornaments, which he had kept safe and said the direction which they had flown. Sugriva promises Rama his assistance in killing Ravana, and Rama promises Sugriva to help him kill Vali, who has banished Sugriva and forcefully took his wife and kingdom. Sugriva tells Rama to overcome his grief as only unwise and distressed get sunk in sorrow.

Sugriva then narrated the story of Vali to Rama, *"Vali was an extremely strong warrior who had developed enmity with demon Mayavi, who challenged him for a duel. I followed Vali due to my affection towards him. The demon ran towards a cave, and both fought for days. I waited outside the cave as Vali instructed. As days passed, I heard only the noise of demons from inside, and I saw a pool of blood flowing from inside; I assumed Vali to be dead. I thereby blocked the entrance of the cave and returned to the kingdom. When all the ministers came to know about this, they decided to coronate me, and I started ruling the kingdom, abiding by the laws. One day after the killing of the demon, Vali returned and saw me sitting on the throne. Assuming I betrayed him, he imprisoned the ministers. Though I bowed to him and tried explaining my side and wanted to hand over the kingdom to him, he was angry. He banished me and took away my wife by force."* Rama assured Sugriva to kill Vali.

As per the plan, Sugriva challenged Vali in a duet, and during the fight, Rama could not distinguish the two. Exhausted and badly beaten by mighty Vali, Sugriva ran to hide. Rama explained to annoyed Sugriva that during the fight, it was impossible to distinguish between the two and hence told to wear necklace of flower gajapushpi around his neck for the next fight. The next day, Sugriva again challenged Vali. Tara, Vali's wife, tried to counsel her husband by telling her to forgive his brother and make a friendship with the great Rama of the Ikshvaku race, who was seen in the forest by their son, Angad. But Vali, ignoring her, went ahead with the duel in which Rama struck Vali with the arrow. On falling to the ground, Vali asked why a righteous king killed him when he was engaged in battle with others.

Rama then replied, *"Bharata rules this land and is the protector of dharma. By his command, we are devoted to upholding dharma. You have violated dharma; you have strayed from the dharma of a king. You are forcefully living with your younger brother's wife, who is virtually like your daughter-in-law. Those who commit sin against own daughter, sister or brother's wife should be killed."* Vali understood his mistake and told Rama to protect Sugriva and Angad. Tara and Angad arrived there crying at the sight of the fallen Vali. He tells Sugriva to take care of Angad as his son and tells him to carry out Rama's task without hesitation. Sugriva and Angad perform the last rites of Vali.

Hanuman Reminded of His Powers

Sugriva is coronated as the king, and Rama says that he has been forbidden from entering any city or village for fourteen years due to a promise given to his father. He stays out in the forest and tells Sugriva to make preparations for killing Ravana during the autumn period. After attaining the kingdom, Sugriva engrossed himself in pleasures, to which Hanuman reminded him of the promise made to Rama. Sugriva commands Angad and Nila to assemble all the warrior monkeys. Meanwhile, Rama, also in agony, sent Lakshmana to remind Sugriva of the promises made. Tara tried to pacify the anger of Lakshaman, who had come to remind Sugriva of his dharma. She tells him to forgive Sugriva's mistake, and Sugriva has already initiated efforts to accomplish their task.

A large number of vanaras from various parts assemble in front of Rama, and Rama expresses his gratitude. Sugriva sends all the vanaras in different directions in search of Sita and Ravana. Hanuman, Nila, Angad and Jambavan proceed southwards. During their search, they meet Sampati, Jatayu's elder brother, who tells Angad that Ravana is on the island of Lanka, down south. Hanuman, Angad, and Jambavan, along with other vanaras, reach the shore of the ocean.

As all the vanaras were discussing their ability to leap the farthest, Jambhavan turned to Hanuman and said, *"O Hanuman, you are superior in strength, wisdom and brilliance. Your strength, speed and valour are equivalent to that of the mighty Garuda. Your mother, Anjana, an apsara by the name of Punjikasthala, was of utmost beauty and was married to Kesari. She was born in our race due to a curse but could assume any shape. Once, when she assumed the form of a beautiful lady and stood on a mountaintop, she was glanced at by Wind God. Being a chaste woman, she was bewildered by what the Wind God said that their union was only in mind. He then told her that soon she would be blessed with a son who would be of great valour and would be able to leap and fly, equalling the wind god. Once assuming the Sun to be fruit, you flew towards the sun to seize it but were stopped by Indra by hurling the weapon vajra at you. You fell on the mountain peak and had your chin broken. Hence, your name is Hanuman. Seeing this, Vayu Dev (wind god) was angry, and to pacify him, Brahma gave you a boon that you will never be struck upon by any weapon. Indra gave you a boon that you will die only when you wish for it. Garuda endowed with valour and courage."* Reminded of his powers, Hanuman leapfrogs across the ocean from the mountain of Mahendra and reaches the shores of Lanka.

Hanuman in Lanka

On reaching Lanka, Hanuman started his search for Sita. He was amazed at the beauty of the palace of Ravana, built by Vishvakarma. Hanuman decided to assume a tiny form and jump into the city during the night to remain undetected by the demons. As Hanuman was entering the gates of the city, the spirit of Lanka, demoness Lankini, obstructed him and hit him. In return, Hanuman assumed a huge form, hit her with a fist, and she fell aground. Being a lady, Hanuman didn't kill her. She then revealed that Lord Brahma had given her a boon that when a vanara hit her, it would signal the destruction of the rakshasas and the kingdom of Lanka. She then allowed Hanuman to enter the city and serve his purpose.

In search of Sita, Hanuman enters the palaces of Ravana, Kumbhakarna, Vibhishana and many others, but in vain. He sees the splendid aerial chariot of Ravana, Pushpaka Vimana, which was built by Vishvakarma and given to his brother Kubera, from whom Ravana forcefully took it. Dejected at not finding Janaki (daughter of King Janaka, Sita), Hanuman enters the garden of Ashoka trees (Ashoka Vatika). There, he saw a woman in soiled clothes, looking dejected and surrounded by demons. Hanuman was pleased as he recognised that the lady was Devi Sita herself, but seeing her in this state, his heart started to weep.

At dawn, unable to control his senses, Ravana comes to Sita and tempts her to be his chief wife and enjoy all the pleasures. He also says there is no one who can save her from his clutches. Sita then replies that she cannot be lured by his power or wealth; she is inseparable from Rama. She tells him to free her and try friendship with Rama, who is compassionate. Otherwise, this action of yours will be the cause of the destruction of the city. Giving an ultimatum to Sita, Ravana tells his guards to pursue Sita to change her mind or face consequences. The demoness tries to convince Sita, but the righteous Sita does not sway.

Hanuman, who had seen and heard all this, devises a plan to approach Sita. He starts singing praises of Rama from the tree under which Sita is sitting. Hanuman then tells the tales of Rama and Lakshmana to Sita, as Sita suspects Hanuman to be Ravana in disguise. He tells Sita that he is the minister of Sugriva and messenger of Shree Rama. Hanuman also shows Rama's ring to Sita and offers to fly her back to Rama on his shoulders. Sita refuses as the percentage of successfully reaching back is uncertain. Hence, she advises it would be better if Hanuman comes with Rama, kills Ravana and takes her back. Sita then gave Hanuman apiece of chudamani worn on her head to Hanuman to be presented to Rama as a mark of identification. Hanuman takes permission to depart.

Chapter 20

Shree Rama: The War of Lanka

Hanuman Tests Ravana

Prior to departing, Hanuman decided to test the strength of Ravana's army, thereby killing a few of the demons; the demons who are proud of their strength would be demoralised. In order to grab Ravana's attention, the mischievous Vanara, Hanuman, assuming a huge form, uprooted the trees in the Ashoka Vatika and devastated the beautiful garden. He then stood at the exit of the doorway, waiting to single-handedly take on a few of the asuras. On being reported to Ravana about the devastation, he sent thousands of demons, "kinkaras", to attack the vanaras. Hanuman made a loud, thunderous noise and hails Rama, thereby killing all of them. After this, he was attacked by the invincible Jambumali, son of Prahstya (maternal uncle of Ravana). He was also killed by Hanuman, which further enraged Ravana, who then sent seven sons of his ministers and later his five generals. During the battle, their bodies started to drop dead one by one while their terrified armies fled away in all directions.

Ravana then glanced at his son Aksha, who was a mighty warrior who was difficult to subdue. Aksh and Hanuman were engaged in a fierce battle, at the end of which Prince Aksha was killed. Ravana then sent his warrior prince, Indrajit, one who could invoke BrahmaAstra (Weapons) to capture Hanuman. A fierce battle again broke out in which none could overpower each other. Finally, Indrajit invoked the Brahmastra. Paying respect to the great weapon of the Creator Brahma and sighting an opportunity to talk to Ravana, Hanuman allowed himself to be tied up by the astra and be brought to the court of Ravana. Hanuman released himself from the binding of Brahmastra but allowed himself to be tied up by rope.

Prahstya, on behalf of King Ravana, enquired about Hanuman and the purpose of his visit. Hanuman replied that he was a vanaras and no astras could subdue him, and it was only with the purpose of meeting Ravana that he allowed himself to be tied up. Also, he informed that he was the messenger of the great Rama. In order to instil fear in the minds of Ravana and another asura, Hanuman told him that he alone could destroy Lanka, but he had not received Rama's permission. Enraged, Ravana ordered to kill Hanuman but was stopped by his righteous brother Vibhishana as Hanuman was an envoy. As a punishment, Ravana orders to put fire on the tail of Hanuman. After his tail was set on fire, Hanuman released himself from the binding and set every house and palace in Lanka, except that of Vibhishana, on fire.

After ensuring Sita is safe, Hanuman returned to Rama and gave the news of safety of Sita. Hanuman hands over Sita's chudamani and narrates the entire episode to Rama. Rama praises Hanuman and gladly embraces him on his successful return. Rama is again struck in grief thinking of his beloved wife. Sugriva consoles him and tells him to be courageous.

Vibhishana Seeks Rama

Hanuman gives a description of Lanka and the fortification of the city. He also describes the strength of Indrajit and Ravana. Rama, who is well respected by everyone, instructs politely to march towards Lanka and assigns duties to various leaders. Soon they reached the shore of the vast sea between their land and Lanka. Assembling there, the mighty warriors discussed the ways to cross the mighty ocean.

Meanwhile, in Lanka, when the mighty Hanuman destroyed their city, Ravana and his councillors discussed how to defeat Rama. All the warriors and ministers assured Ravana that they would be able to overcome Rama, Lakshmana and Sugriva. Among them, the righteous Vibhishana stood up and said, *"It is not good for us to have enmity with powerful warriors and followers of dharma. We have this fear today because, for no reason, Sita is brought here. Give her back to Rama. If Rama's wife is not given, Lanka will be destroyed along with all Rakshasas."* Vibhishana appeals to Ravana again and again to give back Sita to Rama. Disregarding the advice of his younger brother, Ravana orders his minister to prepare to protect the city.

Kumbhakarna, who had completed his six-month sleep, angrily told Ravana that he should have consulted them prior to doing such a sinful act of kidnapping another's wife. Kumbhakarna also said that it was his good fortune that Rama didn't kill Ravana yet. But since this sinful act has already been carried out, Kumbhakarna assured Ravana that he would stand with him and fight the enemy, even though it is a wrongful act.

Vibhishana again tries to convince Ravana but is objected to by Indrajit and Ravana. Enraged, Vibhishana, along with his four Rakshasas, gets up and departs to the northern shore where Vanaras were waiting and wished to meet Rama. Initially, everyone suspected him to be a spy. But on listening to the words of Hanuman and Rama, they accept Vibhishana. On seeing Rama, Vibhishana and the four rakshasas fell at his feet and sought shelter. Vibhishana then described the strength of his brothers

Ravana, Kumbhakarna, Indrajit and all other warriors. Rama assured that after Ravana is killed, Vibhishana will be coronated as king of Rakshasas. Ravana sent Suka to spy on Rama's army but was captured by Vanaras, but Rama says a messenger should never be hurt or killed. Hence, he was held captive.

Crossing the Ocean

At the shores of the ocean, Rama spent three nights fasting for the Lord of the ocean to appear. Since the ocean lord didn't appear, angry Rama put an arrow presided by Brahma on his bow and was ready to release it to dry up the ocean. Lakshmana tried to stop him, and the whole atmosphere turned dark at that moment. Then, the Lord of the ocean appeared and said that he should not release the arrow as, being in its natural state, the ocean could not solidify itself. The ocean then suggested that Vanara Nala, who was the son of Vishvakarma, was capable of building the bridge across the ocean. On getting orders from Rama, Nala acknowledged and ordered the other vanaras to gather huge stones, trees, and logs of wood. Vanaras started dumping huge boulders, trees, creepers, etc., into the water, and Nalas started building the bridge across the ocean. Soon the beautiful bridge, setu across the ocean was ready, and this incredible feat was witnessed by all Devatas.

Vibhishana first crossed the ocean and reached the other side with his mace, to ensure the rakshasas don't destroy the magnificent bridge. Sugriva then requested to Rama to climb on back of Hanuman and Lakshmana on the back of Angad, as they will help them cross the bridge quickly. All the Vanaras soon reached the shores of Lanka. Rama then asked Lakshmana to divide the army of Vanaras into sections.

Sugriva then suggests that Suka be released. Suka then went to Ravana and informed him that Rama and Vanaras had set foot on the Lankan shores. The angry Ravana, praising his own valour, said at any cost, he is not willing to release Sita. Ravana then sends spies Suka and Saarana and then Shardula disguised in the form of Vanara to measure the strength of his enemies. Vibheeshna recognised them, and they were captured and brought before Rama. But Rama, sighting Dharma, releases them. They return to Ravana and describe the might of Rama and Lakshmana. Vibheeshna sends his four ministers inside Lanka in the form of birds to assess Ravana's plans. Vibheeshna then reveals the same to Rama.

Preparation for the Battle

Having heard Rama and his army's valour through his spies, Ravana called on his ministers to discuss the strategies. After this, he went to the trickster, Vidyujihya, to make a false head of Rama. He then went to Sita and told the fake story of Rama's killing and showed her the fake head of Rama. Hearing this, Sita, weeping, fell unconscious. After Ravana left, a female Rakshasa, Saramaa, who had been friendly with Sita, approached her and told them that it was a trick played by Ravana. She also informed her that the valiant Rama and his Vanara army had crossed the ocean and reached the shores of Lanka. Ravana's maternal grandfather, Malyava, suggested Ravana join hands with Rama, who is Vishnu in human form. But Ravana refused to do so.

Meanwhile, Rama instructed Nila to stay at the east gate and fight Prahasta, while the mighty Angada crushed Ravana's leader, Mahaparvasha and Mahodara at the south gate. While Hanuman entered through the west gate, Rama and Lakshmana attacked from the north gate. Sugriva, the great bear Jambhavan and Vibheeshna were to fight Lanka from the middle. Rama and his army then went to the top of the Suvela mountain to have a bird's-eye view of Lanka. Rama and Sugriva caught a glimpse of Ravana. Enraged at his sight, the courageous Sugriva jumped onto the top of the tower and engaged in dual combat with Ravana. After the fierce combat, once Ravana was exhausted, Sugriva returned. Rama then told Sugriva he should refrain from such acts as if anything undue happened to Sugriva, he would not be able to bear it.

After they descended from the mountain, each team occupied its position. Rama summons Angad and sends him as a messenger to Ravana's court. He tells him that if Ravana seeks Rama's protection and handovers Sita back, he will leave without a fight. Otherwise, the city of Lanka would be devastated. Hearing Rama's message from the son of Vali, Ravana was enraged and ordered his ministers to catch him. Showing a glimpse of his valour, he threw away the Rakshasas, broke the palace's roof, and flew back to Rama. Helpless Ravana could only watch this. Ravana ordered his forces to advance in the night. Retaliating to it, Rama ordered the vanaras to attack as they laid siege to Lanka. A fierce battle broke out between the Vanaras alongside bears led by Sugriva and Jambhavan and the Rakshasas.

The Battle Begins

As the battle broke out, warriors from both sides started hitting each other with various weapons. The great Vanara, Sushena, dropped a huge rock on the Rakshasa Vidyunmali and killed him. Angad destroyed Indrajit's chariot with his mace. As the night began to set in, the Rakshasas grew stronger. Rama, with his mighty skills, destroyed many of the mighty Ravana's warriors. Indrajit, the great illusionist, disappeared after being struck and defeated by Angad. He became angry and, in his invisible form, shot repeatedly the arrows of serpents all over Rama and

Lakshmana's bodies. Due to the relentless attack by invisible and deceitful Indrajit using the venomous serpent arrow, the two mighty princes fell and were lying on the battlefield covered with arrows. Indrajit, after the attack, left the scene, presuming them to be dead.

The Vanaras, seeing their heroes fallen, were tragic-struck. Vibheeshna, Sugriva, Hanuman, Angad, and all other warriors assembled there and saw Rama and Lakshmana drenched in blood, lying in a bed of serpent arrows. Indrajit attacked all other Vanara leaders also and, presuming the death of Rama and Lakshmana, felt happy and entered the city as he had won the day's battle. He gave this news to his father, Ravana. Ravana ordered the Rakshasa guards to take Sita and Trijata in his pushpak viman and show her the bodies of dead Rama and Lakshmana. As Sita was flying over the site, she saw the bodies of Rama and Lakshmana lying on the ground surrounded by Vanaras, and she started weeping and lamenting. Then Trijata told her that the bodies of Rama and Lakshmana were being guarded by Vanara, which indicates that Rama and Lakshmana were not dead. She assured Sita that it was impossible for anyone to kill them.

On gaining consciousness and seeing Lakshmana bound and injured, Rama was stuck in grief. As Sushena was discussing medicinal herbs to be brought by Hanuman for curing Lakshmana, a strong wind started to blow across the place, uprooting all the trees in the vicinity. Suddenly, from the clouds of dust and strong breeze, the mighty Garuda, the son of Vinatha, flapped its huge wings. Seeing Garuda, all the serpents in the form of arrows bound on Rama and Lakshmana fled away. Miraculously, all wounds on their body, too, disappeared. Garuda and Rama paid respect to each other. After embracing Rama, Garuda soared back to the sky. The Vanara troops rejoiced and entered the city again with renewed energy.

Hearing the news of Rama and Lakshmana being alive, Ravana sends Dhumraksha to kill them, but he was slained by the mighty Hanuman using the peak of a mountain. Ravana then sent Vajradhamshtra, who was killed by Angad. Hanuman then killed Akampana, who was sent by Ravana. Ravana then sends his Commander-in-Chief, Prahastha, to destroy the army of Sugriva. As the army of Prahasta attacked the Vanaras, Dwividha killed Rakshasa Naranthaka, Vanara Dhurmukha killed Rakshasa Samunnata, Jambhavan killed Mahanada and Tara killed the Rakshasa Kumbhahanu. While mighty Prahasta was killing and attacking Vanaras, Nila, though wounded by his arrows, attacked and killed Prahasta.

With all his mighty warriors being killed one by one, Ravana entered the war and attacked various Vanara leaders. He is attacked first by Sugriva, who, hurt by Ravana, falls down. Hanuman attacks Ravana with his fist, and seeing his valour, Ravana sped away from him. He then engaged in a fierce battle with Neel, who attacked Ravana but, in the end, was hurt by him. Lakshaman then fought Ravana but was hit by Ravana's spear. Hanuman then rescued Lakshmana and told Rama to climb on his back and fight Ravana. Rama climbed on the back of Hanuman and destroyed Ravana's chariot and weapons. Rama then hit Ravana's crown and dislodged it from his head, thereby denting his pride. Rama tells Ravana to rest and come back again. Ravana hastily returns after being defeated by Rama.

End of Kumbhakarna

With his ego and pride badly battered, Ravana sat on his throne in fear and started to think that he should have included even humans when asking for the boon of immunity from Lord Brahma. He also remembered the curse from Ikshvaku King

Anaranya, which said that a man born from his race would kill him, and it seems to be coming true. He also saw the curse of Vedavati and many other women, whose modesty he tried to violate, seems to be coming true. Stuck in fear, Ravana ordered to wake up the huge Kumbhakarna, who, after discussing with Ravana, had gone to sleep nine days back. The Rakshasas went to the palace of Kumbhakarna with a variety of meat and garlands to wake him up. They tried to play loud music and also beat him to wake him up. A large number of elephants were made to walk on his huge body. Suddenly, he woke up from his sleep with a roar and ate all the items that were kept in front of him. Kumbhakarna then asked the reason for the untimely waking him up. Rakshasas then narrated the whole episode of the ongoing war to him.

Rama enquired about the gigantic Rakshasa, Kumbhakarna to Vibheeshna. He replied, *"Kumbhakarna was born powerful, unlike other Rakshasas who received their power through boons. As he was born hungry and huge, he started consuming all beings in his sight. All people, out of fear, sought the help of Indra, who tried to hurt Kumbhakarna with his Vajra, but Kumbhakarna pulled out the tusk of Indra's Airvavata and struck Indra. All Devatas and people then approached Lord Brahma for help, who cursed Kumbhakarna to fall asleep. At the request of Ravana, Kumbhakarna's curse was reduced, and Lord Brahma told Kumbhakarna that he would sleep for 6 months and wake up for a day, and on that day, he would eat as much as he could. Overtaken by fear of defeat from you, Ravana had woken up Kumbhakarna."* Rama then ordered Neel to organise the army and be ready with all weapons.

On reaching the palace of Ravana, Kumbhakarna was told by Ravana that he needed his help to destroy the Vanaras who had attacked them. Kumbhakarna reminded Ravana that he was reaping the fruits of the sinful act he had committed.

ॐ

Hearing Kumbhakarna's advice, Ravana got agitated. On seeing him agitated, Kumbhakarna consoled him and told him he would kill Rama and his tormentors. Kumbhakarna departed, and seeing his huge body, the vanaras were frightened and began to run helter-skelter. Angad then restored confidence in them, and they began to attack Kumbhakarna. Kumbhakarna, with his mighty size and strength, destroyed many Vanaras. Hanuman and Angad did manage to injure Kumbhakarna. Lakshmana then displayed his valour and was praised by Kumbhakarna. But told them he wished to fight only Rama.

Kumbhakarna, upon seeing Rama, challenged him for dual. Rama showered arrows at Kumbhakarna, but none had any effect or induce pain on Kumbhakarna. Then, using the weapon, Vayvyam severed the right arm, which fell on the vanaras, killing them. Kumbhakarna then hauled huge trees at Rama with his left hand. Then, using the IndrAstra, Rama severed his left hand, which further crushed many Rakshasas and Vanaras. Kumbhakarna screamed in agony and rushed towards Rama; Rama, using a crescent moon-shaped arrow, cut his legs. As Kumbhakarna used his huge mouth to suck in everything in his vicinity, Rama filled his mouth with arrows, and the huge Rakshasa, unable to speak, fainted. Rama, using the weapon of Lord Brahma and chanting Indra's mantra, discharged an arrow that severed Kumbhakarna's head, thereby killing him. Vanaras rejoiced at the sight, and upon hearing this, Ravana was immersed in grief. He started to think that he had no purpose in life and didn't need Sita anymore. But thought that he must avenge the death of Kumbhakarna.

Ravana's son came forward to console him and expressed their desire to enter the battle and kill Rama. They, along with the army and Ravana's brother, attacked the vanaras, but the Rakshasa troops were overpowered by vanaras. Naranthaka, Ravana's son, was killed by the mighty Angad in a fistfight as he was destroying the vanaras. Seeing Naranthaka killed, the other sons, Trishira, Devanthaka and Mahodara, charged at Angad but were valiantly resisted by Angad. Hanuman and Neel set out to help Angad. Although severely injured by Ravana's brother, Mahodara, Neel managed to kill him, while Hanuman killed Trishira and Devanthaka. Rshaba, the mighty Vanara, though injured, killed Ravana's brother Mahaparshva.

Hearing this, Atikaya, son of Ravana and Dhanyamalini, entered the battlefield and soon met Lakshmana, and a fierce battle of arrows began. None of Lakshmana's arrows could pierce the body of Atikaya. Then Vayu (Wind God) told Lakshmana that due to a boon by Lord Brahma, Atikaya's body is covered by impenetrable armour, and he can only be slayed by the BrahmAstra. So, Lakshmana invoked the BrahmAstra, placed it on his bow, and released it. The great weapon severed Atikaya's head and killed him.

Killing of Indrajit

Hearing the news of the death of his sons and brothers, Ravana's eyes were filled with tears. He was concerned about the kingdom. Indrajit, the foremost son of Ravana, came foreward and told him that he will kill Rama and Lakshmana. He, taking the blessing of his father, departs on his chariot to the battlefield. Enraged and in his invisible form, he showered arrows and injured all the Vanara leaders. With the boon of invincibility given to him by Lord Brahma, Indrajit showered arrows on Rama and Lakshmana. Soon, both of them were badly injured and fell unconscious. Vanaras immediately withdrew them from the battlefield. Vibheeshna consoled them by saying they had fallen, paying respect to the arrows presided over Brahma, which were hurled upon them by Indrajit. Hanuman and Vibheeshna tried to restore confidence in the vanaras, including Sugriva, Angada and others who were struck down by Indrajit. Jambhavan enquired about Hanuman and said if Hanuman is alive, there is hope for everyone.

Jambhavan, the wise bear, calls upon Hanuman and instructs him, *"O hero Hanuman, you ought to fly to the Himalayas and in between the two mountains, Rshabha and Kailasa is a splendid mountain of medicinal herbs. There on top, you will see medicinal herbs illuminating in all directions – Mritasanjivani (capable of restoring life), Vishalyakarani (capable of healing wounds), Suvarnakarani (restoring original complexion) and Sandhaani (capable of joining bones). You need to bring them back urgently and restore the life and injuries of all fallen."*

Hearing this, Hanuman, with the speed of the wind, reached the Himalayas, saw the abodes frequented by Devatas and started searching for herbs. Perceived by the seeker, all the herbs disappeared and enraged Hanuman roared and uprooted the mountain and hurried back to Lanka. Having placed the mountain peak in the midst of the vanara army, Hanuman embraced Vibheeshna. Inhaling the fragrance of herbs, both the princes became free of wounds. After that, vanara heroes were also restored, and so were other vanara warriors. Ravana had ordered Rakshasas to dump the bodies of dead Rakshasas in the ocean so that vanaras wouldn't have a count of the dead ones. After this, Hanuman, with his mighty speed, quickly carried away the mountain back to the Himalayas and came back to join Rama in the battle of Lanka.

Rejuvenated vanaras started setting fire to the gates and prepared for battle. Ravana then sent Kumbhakarna's sons, Kumbha and Nikumbha, along with others, for the battle. Angada killed Kampana and Prajaghna, Dwivida killed Sonitaksha, Mainda killed Yupaksha, while Sugriva killed Kumbha in a fierce battle.

Hanuman then killed Nikumbha. Hearing the death of Kumbha and Nikumbha, Makarakshah, son of Ravana's brother Khara, showered the arrow on the vVanaras, but he too was killed by Rama's arrow.

Indrajit again entered the battle after offering his fire sacrifice, and by being invisible, he again showered arrows on Rama and Lakshmana. Lakshmana wanted to use BrahmAstra but was stopped by Rama, as it would also destroy many innocent Rakshasas. The evil-minded Indrajit created an illusionary Sita and placed her on his chariot. Hanuman saw the illusionary Sita and rushed towards Indrajit. Indrajit took out his sword, severed the head of Sita in front of them, and sped away to Nikumbhilam, the sacrificial ground to perform yajna. Hanuman, in grief, gave the news of Sita's killing to Rama, who fell unconscious.

Vibheeshna then consoles Rama, saying Ravana would never kill Sita and that it was only Indrajit's illusionary Sita. He did this trick to keep everyone away till he completed the ritual at Nikumbhilam. On completion of this ritual, it will not be possible to defeat him. Indrajit could only be killed when he has not performed sacrifice at Nikumbhilam. Lakshmana, accompanied by Vibheeshna, Hanuman, Angada and other vanaras, reaches Nikumbhilam and attacks the guarding Rakshasas so that Indrajit is visible. Indrajit, on hearing the cries of his men, got up without completing the rituals and saw Hanuman destroying his people. As per Vibheeshna's advice, Lakshmana entered into a fierce battle with Indrajit and both of them were severely wounded and bathed in blood. In the fight, the charioteer was killed, and vanaras killed his horses. Finally, using the IndrAstra, Lakshmana severed the head of Indrajit from his body, thereby killing him. Rejoiced, Lakshmana, Vibheeshna and the rest reached Rama, where Sushena treated Lakshmana's wounds.

The Final Battle

Lamenting over the loss of Indrajit, Ravana decides to kill Sita but is stopped by his minister Suparshva. Ravana sends his huge army to attack Rama, but it is destroyed by Rama's ferocious showers of arrows. All the wives of dead Rakshasas cry over the death of their husbands and cursed the ugly lady, Shurpanaka, who they believe is the cause of such mass destruction. Ravana then sends his army generals to war and followed them to show his might. The army generals and his armies were killed and destroyed by Sugriva and Angad.

A fierce battle of arrows broke out between the Great Rama and Evil Ravana. During the fight, Vibheeshna killed Ravana's horses. While attempting to save the life of Vibheeshna, Lakshaman was severely injured in his chest by Ravana's spear. Enraged by this, Rama hurled arrows that the Rakshasas and Ravana could not withstand, and they fled away. Rama was grieved by Lakshmana, who had fallen unconscious. Rama was consoled by Sushena, who told Hanuman to get the herbs Savaranyakarni, Sanjeevakarani, Sandhaani, and Sarvakarni. Hanuman flew immediately to the mountain, unable to recognise the herb, and to prevent loss of time, brought the mountain at high speed. Sushena picked the needed herbs, crushed them, and dropped the extract into Lakshmana's nose. Lakshmana stood up, and all vanaras and Rama rejoiced.

Ravana ascended on another chariot and attacked Rama, who was standing on Earth. Indra, on seeing this, sent his chariot and charioteer, Mathali, along with his weapons, to Rama. Various dreadful weapons were discharged by both. With an array of arrows being showered, Ravana's charioteer withdrew the chariot from the battlefield, but Ravana scolded him to get back to the battlefield. Meanwhile, Rishi Agastya, who was watching the battle along with Devatas, gave the secret mantra, "Aditya hridayam", *to* Shree Rama for the victory. A fierce duel resumed between the two warriors that lasted for seven days and nights. Rama cut off Ravana's head, but a similar-looking second head rose, which was cut off again immediately. As soon as one is cut off, another head rose. Mathali then reminded Rama of the BrahmAstra. Rama, fixing the great arrow on the bow and fully stretching, released the arrow at great speed. Arrow penetrating the chest of Ravana and killing him, and having accomplished the task, the arrow returned to the quiver.

With Rakshasa king killed, all Rakshasa fled, and vanaras, Devatas, Sugriva, and all other warriors started to rejoice. Seeing his brother die, Vibheeshna was immersed in sorrow but was consoled by Rama. All wives, including the excellent Mandodari, start to cry seeing their husbands lying dead. The women were lamenting, *"He, who could not be killed by Devatas, Danavas, Rakshasas, asuras or Yakshas, such a hero lies lifeless, killed by a mortal who came by walk. You didn't listen to anyone and brought Sita here with evil intentions and destroyed yourself and all of us."* Vibheeshna then performed Ravana's last rites after Rama requested them.

Chapter 21

Shree Rama:
The Ideal King

Sita Agni-Pareeksha

The Devatas, Gandharvas, Danavas were praising Rama's prowess, end of evil Ravana, valour of Hanuman, love of Lakshmana, faithfulness of Sita and loyalty of vanaras. Rama then consecrated the righteous Vibheeshna and became the king of Lanka. The citizens were pleased with the decision.

Rama told Hanuman to get permission from Vibheeshna to enter Lanka, enquire about her well-being, and return with her words. Hanuman acknowledged Rama and took permission from Vibheeshna to enter Lanka and reach Sita. Hanuman communicated the news of Rama's victory. He also wished to kill the Rakshasas who threatened her. Sita, hearing the words, had no words to speak out of joy and also told Hanuman to forgive the demoness as they had done only under the command of their king. She also desired to see Rama. Hanuman quickly went back and gave the message.

Rama, on hearing this, shedding tears of joy, said to Vibheeshna to bring Sita. As per Rama's request, Sita was brought in a palanquin, bathed and anointed with ornaments. Rama, upon seeing Sita, experienced joy, anger, and misery at the same time. Rama spoke to Vibheeshna to allow Sita to be brought before him by walking and not by palanquin. Astonished by Rama's statement, Sugriva, Lakshmana and Hanuman became highly distressed and thought that Rama was displeased with Sita. Rama, upon seeing Sita, the one who was dear to him, was burning inside with fear of public opinion. Rama then described the efforts that were made to succeed in the war and thereby said he had removed the indignity that he had lost and then, with great discomfort, said, *"With your virtue in doubtful state, you standing in front of me is extremely disagreeable to me, even as a light to one who is suffering from poor eyesight.* (Rama tactically blamed those who laid doubt about Sita's purity by saying that one with poor eyesight cannot see the brightness of light). *I am permitting you to go wherever you like. I have no work with you. You may go to the place of your choice."*

Sita, dejected on hearing these horrible words from her beloved Rama, was dejected and said, *"Why are you addressing me in such a rude manner? I am not as you think, if so show me proof of that from the past. You should give up judging all women by the path followed by vulgar women. When Ravana contacted me, I was helpless and was against my will. My fate is to be blamed and not me. My mind is under my control, and my heart always beats for you. You also gave up yourself to anger like a weak man and adopted womanliness."* She looked at Lakshmana and told him to arrange a burning pyre for her. Lakshmana looked at Rama, understanding his expression, and prepared the pyre. Sita went towards the pyre and said, *"If my heart has never gone away from Rama or if I am of impeccable character, or if I have never been unfaithful to Rama, may the fire god protect me."* Saying this, Sita went around the fire and, free from any hesitation, entered the burning fire.

Everyone assembled there, including the Devatas, Gandharvas, Danavas, Rakshasas, and Vanaras, witnessed this. Rama's eyes were filled with tears. Lord Brahma then reminded

Rama that he was the incarnation of Vishnu, and Sita was Devi Lakshmi.

Agni Devata (Fire God) in his human form emerged from the fire along with Janaka's daughter, unhurt, adorned with ornaments and presented her to Rama and told him that Sita was without any sin, auspicious and faithful by speech or glance or by thought. The Supreme Rama rejoiced and told Lord Brahma, *"I am aware that Sita is without any sin, purest, and her love is undivided and devoted to me. She is capable of protecting herself. Sita is no different from me, and I would not be able to renounce her. Having stayed in Ravana's place, people might think that Rama has accepted her out of lust, if not tested. Only to convince the world, I allowed her to enter the fire. No one can access or lay thoughts in her mind."* Saying this, Rama, of great strength, experiencing great joy, reunited with his beloved Sita. Lord Shiva delivered the auspicious message to Rama about the killing of Ravana, thereby relieving the world of his fear. Lord Shiva then brings Dasharatha to Rama, Sita and Lakshmana, who blesses them and thereafter returns to the abode of God.

Return to Ayodhya

Happy at the turn of events and the killing of Ravana, Indra, with joined hands, enquired Rama about his desire. Rama then requests him to bring back the life of all bears and vanaras who lost their life in war. All the vanaras and bears duly healed, enriched with strength, rose from death. On Vibheeshna's request to stay for a few more days, Rama said as the day of exile is almost over, he is longing to meet Bharata. He then thanked Vibheeshna for his hospitality and friendship and requested permission to return. Vibheeshna offered his Pushpak Viman so that they could return to Ayodhya in a day. He also rewarded the vanaras, who had fought brilliantly during the epic battle.

Vibheeshna, Sugriva, and other vanaras also desired to go to Ayodhya with Rama to meet Kaushalya. Rama was very pleased to hear this. Rama, Lakshmana, Sita, along with Vibheeshna, his ministers and other vanaras, seated in the beautifully decorated aerial chariot and flew towards Ayodhya. Enroute, upon seeing the beautiful kingdom of Kishkinda, Sita wished Tara and other wives of Sugriva to accompany them to Ayodhya. So, at Rama's request, Sugriva also invited all of them.

Rama made his stop at the hermitage of Sage Bharadwaja and paid him homage. Rama instructed Hanuman to check the well-being of his people, then go to Srigaberipuram and meet Guha, the King of Nishadas and enquire about his well-being. Further to this Rama instructed Hanuman to meet Bharata and inform him about his arrival and narrate the incidents that occurred during the exile. Hanuman quickly met Guha and then Bharata, living in a hermitage, and narrated everything to him. The magnificent Bharata, overwhelmed with joy, embraced Hanuman and ordered Shatrughna to make all preparations for his dear brother's arrival.

As Pushpak Viman descended at Ayodhya, Bharata offered respect to Rama with joined hands. Rama embraced Bharata and lifted him; Bharata then approached Lakshmana and greeted Sita. Bharata then embraced Sugriva, Jambhavan, Angad, Mainda, Dwivida, Nila, Rishabh, Sushena, Nala and all other vanaras. Shatrughna also greeted everyone. Rama then met his mothers, Kaushalya, Sumitra and Kaikeyi and offered them respect. All citizens in joy shouted slogans of Rama.

Rama's Coronation

Taking sandals given to Bharata, he placed them at the feet of Rama and, with folded hands, spoke, *"Here I return the kingdom* _entrusted to me by you. I have accomplished the goal of my life by seeing you return as the king of Ayodhya_". Hearing this, Vibheeshna and the Vanaras eyes filled with tears. Rama was pleased and instructed Pushpak Viman to go to Kubera while he greeted Sage Vasishta and paid the oblation. Bharata then requested Rama to be coronated as the king.

Bharata and Shatrughna helped in getting Rama and Lakshmana ready by cutting their matted hair and decorating them with ornaments. Kaushalya, Kaikeyi and Sumitra helped Sita get ready. The thrilled Kaushalya also decorated the wives of vanaras. Sage Vasishta and ministers prepared whatever was necessary for the grand occasion. All the vanaras on being instructed by Sugriva brought the holy water from all over the land. Vibheeshna, vanara leaders and all other vanaras were richly gifted by Rama.

On the great day, accompanied by the sound of conches and drums, Rama arrived. Rama received blessings from elders. Thus began the ceremony of coronation. Rama narrated the stories of the friendship and valour of vanaras and Vibheeshna to his ministers. The coronation of the greatest King was completed in a grand style. Bharata was assigned the role of Yuvaraj (Prince).

Rama performed various yajnas along with his brothers and friends. Rama of great glory ruled for many years with Lakshmana as his follower. During Rama's reign, there was no sorrow, disease, or thieves, and no harm was done to young people. All people were happy and followed the righteous path. Strictly observing the vow of one woman, leading a royal but pious life, and strictly observing his dharma as a king, Rama led a model life to the world. By her deep love, obedience, pious character, and discipline, Sita had captured Rama's heart.

Sita Reaches Valmiki's Hermitage

One fine day after performing the duties of the king, Rama spent a beautiful time with his beloved and pregnant Sita in his garden. There, she expressed a desire to spend time in the hermitage near the banks of the Ganga. Rama had agreed to fulfil her desires.

As a routine, King Rama sent out his spies to enquire about the state of his citizens and well-being and get feedback on his way of ruling the kingdom. They returned and said that they were proud of Rama's victory over Ravana but were unhappy about Rama bringing back Sita, who had been abducted by Ravana and spent time in Ravana's castle. Since the people have to follow the path of their king, they have to tolerate the same state with regard to their wives, who might be immoral. Rama called upon Bharata, Lakshmana and Shatrughna to discuss the matter.

Rama said that the most chaste Sita was brought back to Ayodhya only after she had testified in the presence of Devatas and Gandharvas for her pure conduct, and he does not have any doubts regarding Sita. Rama had told Bharata to cut off his head to prevent public scandal, or he might have to abandon Sita. With deep grief, considering various options of even leaving the kingdom along with Sita, he finally decided to leave Sita under the care of Valmiki. He did so to preserve the grace of his dearest wife, Sita. If Rama had also left the kingdom with her, it would have been like betraying his kingdom and also would have brought great shame to the entire race. Rama, following his Rajyadharma (duty towards his nation) and keeping the welfare of his people above his personal interests, stayed back. At Rama's order, Lakshmana took Sita to Valmiki's hermitage and left her under the care of the Sage.

It was at Valmiki's ashram, Sita gave birth to two excellent sons – Lava and Kusha, who gained their education under

Valmiki. Rama kept his vow and never married anyone else. For the occasion or any austerities to be performed for the sake of kingdom where presence of wife beside was required, Rama had got a golden statue of Sita built to be placed beside him.

Sage Bhrigu's Curse on MahaVishnu

Once, during a conflict between Devatas and Asuras, the Daityas, threatened by Devatas, took refuge with the wife of Sage Bhrigu. As the wife had given them protection, Devatas took the help of MahaVishnu. MahaVishnu requested Bhrigu's wife, Khyati, to release the Daityas, but she didn't. MahaVishnu tried convincing her against misusing her power, which she had accumulated by severe austerities performed through many years, for unduly protecting the asuras. With no other option, using Sudarshnacharka, MahaVishnu severed the head of Khyati.

Sage Bhrigu who came to place later, on knowing about the incident, cursed MahaVishnu that he would take birth as human and will be separated from his dear wife for very long time. Later having overcome the grief, Bhrigu released his mistake, said that MahaVishnu will incarnate as Maryadapurushottam Rama to undergo the effect of the curse.

Shatrughna Kills Asur Lavana

Once, there was an Asura named Madhu, who had carried out great penance, and as a reward, he obtained a trident from Lord Shiva. Shiva then said as long as he doesn't hurt any innocent or God, the trident would remain with him, and if anyone provokes you, he would be reduced to ashes by the trident. Madhu wished the trident to remain in his family; Lord Shiva said as he pleased with Madhu, he would allow the trident to remain with his son, who would be victorious as long as the trident was in his hands. Madhu and his illustrious wife, Kumbhinasi, bore a cruel son, Lavana. As Lavana grew older, Madhu handed over the trident to him.

Once, sages assembled at Rama's court and requested his help as Lavana was terrorising them. Shatrughna requested that Rama allow him to carry out the duty; Rama, pleased with him, said after killing Lavana, he may establish his kingdom there. At the gates of Madhupura, Shatrughna, on seeing Lavana, challenged him for combat. As Lavana did not have his trident in his hand, he asked Shatrughna to allow him to get his weapon. But Shatrughna said he cannot allow his rival to escape. On hearing this, egoistic Lavana engaged in a fight with Shatrughna, and finally, Lavana was killed by the mighty Shatrughna.

Having killed Lavana, Devata Agni blessed Shatrughna by building the beautiful city of Mathura on the banks of Yamuna. Shatrughna was established as the king of this prosperous kingdom, which was devoid of draught or famines.

Sita Descends to Mother Earth

In due course, Lakshmana had two sons – Angada and Chandraketu, while Bharata's sons were Taksha and Pushkela. The sons of Shatrughna were Subahu and Shrutasena. Once Rama decides to carry out Ashvamedha Yajna, and invites all great people, including Sugriva and other warrior vanaras, along with Vibheeshna. As this sacrifice was being performed, Valmiki arrived there with Lava and Kusha and instructed them to sing Ramayana, which he had taught them, paying full respect to Shree Rama. After listening to the wonderful composition of Valmiki, unheard till then, Rama was greatly astonished. Having recognised his sons, Rama sent for Sita. Rama also summoned all the people, Valmiki, Devatas and other sages.

The next day in the assembly, Rama, wishing to be one with Sita, said that he accepts Lava and Kusha as his sons and asks Sita's pardon and says he never for a moment in his life had doubted her. He also said that he had abandoned her following the duties of the king. He wished to unite with her once again. In her defence, Sita, with joined palms, eyes lowered, said, *"If, even in my thought, I never moved away from Rama, even for a moment, let the Goddess Dharani receive me."*

As these words were being spoken from the earth, rose Goddess Dharani embraced Devi Sita. Showers of flowers fell from the sky. The entire assembly then witnessed Sita descend into the earth as a great tremor passed throughout. In grief and anger, Rama wanted to plough the earth and destroy it to regain Sita. Lord Brahma then reminds Rama of his divine origin, the incarnation of MahaVishnu. Rama spent the days lamenting over the loss of his beloved wife.

As the years passed and spending time with their sons and grandsons, Kaushalya passed away, followed by Sumitra and then Kaikeyi.

End of the Great Era

Rama, helped by Bharata and Shatrughna, established the city of Angadiya for Lakshmana's son Angada and Mallas for Chandrakanta.

One day, Yama visited Rama and told him that he wished to speak with him in private with the condition that no one even overhear the same and if anyone interfered, he must be put to death. Rama told Lakshmana to guard the door so that no one entered the chamber. Yama then told Rama that having accomplished the task in the mortal world, it was time for him to return to the abode of Lord Vishnu.

Meanwhile, Sage Durvasa came to the palace to meet Rama but was stopped by Lakshmana. Afraid of being cursed, Lakshmana entered Rama's chamber while the discussion with Yama was still ongoing. Rama took leave of Yama and paid respect to Sage Durvasa and, on Sage's request, provided him food, after which he returned. Since Lakshmana had intervened in the conversation with Yama, Rama, with a heavy heart, banished Lakshmana, which was equivalent to death for a man of his honour. Lakshmana, on reaching the banks of River Sarayu, performed penance while flowers showered from heaven. He gave up his body in the river.

Rama wished to hand over the kingdom to Bharata and wanted to retire to the forest and follow the path of Lakshmana, but Bharata refused as he, too, wanted to follow Rama. Agreeing with this, Rama installed Kusha as king of the southern region and Lava as king of the northern region. He also summoned Shatrughna, Sugriva, and other vanara leaders, as well as Vibheeshna. Shatrughna, installing his sons as his heir, immediately reached Ayodhya and wished to follow Rama. Sugriva installed Angad as his heir and wished to follow Rama. Rama told Vibheeshna to govern the kingdom of Lanka with justice as long as the people spoke of him. Hanuman said that as long as Rama's name is spoken in this world, he will continue to live according to Rama's will. Jambhavan was also instructed to remain in this mortal world.

Rishis and Gandharvas, along with their children, also wished to follow Rama. All citizens and Vanaras, having bathed and purified of their sins during the Mahaprasthana performed by

ॐ

Sage Vasishta, followed Rama. Following Rama, with the sound of musical instruments and singing by Gandharvas and flowers showering from heaven, Rama, his younger brothers, Rishis, Gandharvas, and all the people entered the waters of River Sarayu. Vishnu and his brothers reached the abode of MahaVishnu, and Sugriva reached Surya. All beings who entered water with Rama, having abandoned their mortal bodies, attained heaven. All Vanaras and bears, who were manifestations of Devatas, returned to the world of Devatas. Thus comes the end of Ramayana, revered by Lord Brahma and written by Sage Valmiki. Lava and Kusha carried forward the legacy of the Ikshvaku race.

Epilogue

The Relevance of Ramayana

Ramayana: The Essence of Purushartha

Ramayana is not just a story, but it is our Itihaasa – that which happened, i.e. our history. It is the epic written by Maharishi Valmiki, which brings out the rules, traditions, and morals of humanity and forms the base of Sanatana Dharma. Ramayana is about a man who is illustrious, pure, righteous, truthful and respectful of elders. The life of Sita is an example of how a woman, a daughter, a wife and a queen should be, and she is an epitome of faithfulness, purity and womanhood. The essence of Purushartha – Dharma, Artha, Kama and Moksha could be splendidly visualised in Rama's life story.

In the modern world, Dharma has taken a backstage in everything. Dharma refers to the code of conduct of a person with regard to individual, family or society. Blindly aping the western society, the traditional values of a family are on the decline. The values of Rama, who chooses to sacrifice the throne of Ayodhya to keep the words of his father, are the ones that need to be followed. Ramayana shows the world the true values of family, respect for elders and their gurus, and the relationship that should exist between siblings. In today's world, where brothers and sisters are ready to slay each other for property, the relationship between Rama and Bharata, Rama and Lakshmana, should provide a role model.

Ravana was a very highly learned man but was overcome by desires and ego, which eventually led to his downfall. In contrast, Rama, following the path of truth and righteousness, experienced divinity. He was faced with many challenges and options to enjoy his life, but he was never caught in the web of desires. The purpose of man doesn't lie in running after materialistic desires. Understanding Purushartha will provide true meaning to life. In Bhagavad Gita, Shree Krishna told Arjuna (Chapter 3, Verse 37, 39):

काम एष क्रोध एष रजोगुणसमुद्भवः ।

महाशनो महापाप्मा विद्ध्येनमिह वैरिणम् ॥

आवृतं ज्ञानमेतेन ज्ञानिनो नित्यवैरिणा ।

कामरूपेण कौन्तेय दुष्पूरेणानलेन च ॥

This means, *"It is the desire, born out of anger in association with mode of passion (Rajo guna), the cause of great sins and the greatest enemy of the world. This desire and anger cover the knowledge of even the most learned person and is like an all-consuming fire."*

The Story of Love and Inspirations

All characters of Ramayana mirror the true human virtues and vices and their outcome. It also showcases two types of kings and his kingdom – Rama and Ayodhya on one side, with Ravana and Lanka on other side. The story of Ramayana is also the story of Hanuman, who served selflessly and with true devotion.

Today, people read Ramayana but never try to understand the essence of it. Even those who read the Ramayana, there are very few who truly follow the teachings. Then there are people who criticise the same without understanding the entire context.

Ravana could not translate his knowledge into action, while Rama, using his knowledge, was able to be the most righteous one – Maryada Purushottam. One must face many challenges in life, but that should be a reason to waver from the goal.

The story of Rama inspires positive energy, one that destroys the destructive elements in a person. Rama is the pride of India, a king who established Rama Rajya, where the duties of a ruler were taught. The life of Rama symbolises righteousness and dharma. Rama was an ideal student, an ideal son, an ideal husband, an ideal brother, an ideal friend and above all, an ideal king. Similarly, Sita was an ideal daughter, an ideal daughter-in-law, an ideal wife, an ideal mother, and above all, a strong, ideal woman. Lakshmana, Bharata, and Shatrughna showed what it means to follow the righteous path and have true brotherly love. Hanuman signifies true devotion, a devotion without any expectation. The bonding between characters enlightens us on how true friendship can be a source of strength and a guiding light.

The story of Ramayana is the path of light to the modern world and to the generations to come. In a world filled with so much depression, stress, anger and materialistic desires, Ramayana is the guiding torch to elevate oneself above them. The timeless wisdom shown in Ramayana should help a man live a virtuous life. It teaches us the importance of our duties and responsibilities, the importance of loyalty and giving respect to every individual. In Valmiki Ramayana 3.9.31 and 3.9.32, it is quoted,

"Dharma brings Artha(wealth), happiness, and everything a person needs. Dharma is the essence of this world. The wise men earn dharma by following various disciplines through great effort and undergoing severe stress. Dharma cannot be achieved by going after materialistic pleasures."

References

My foremost acknowledgement is to Maharishi Valmiki, the author of the greatest epic poem, Ramayana. His poem has been an inspiration for generations. Further to Ramayana, the stories in this book have also been inspired by Hindi and English translations of various. The Puranas which I have referred to here include:

1. Agni Purana
2. Brahma Purana
3. Devi Bhagavata Purana
4. Linga Purana
5. Markandeya Purana
6. Padma Purana
7. Shreemad Bhagavad Purana
8. Vishnupuranam

In addition to the above-mentioned Puranas, Mahabharata and Raghuvamsham by Kalidasa was also referred to for compiling the chapters included in the book.